Ask Your Father

Ask Your Father

EMMA COOK

First published in 2009 by

Short Books

3A Exmouth House

Pine Street

EC1R 0JH

10 9 8 7 6 5 4 3 2 1

A CIP catalogue record for this book
is available from the British Library.

ISBN 978-1-906021-61-0

Printed in Great Britain by CPI Bookmarque, Croydon, CR0 4TD

To Louis and Evie

CONTENTS

INTRODUCTION

'Mummy, why did you write this book?'

The questions began when my son turned three, closely followed by his younger sister and, four years later, they're still at it. 'Mum, why can't we live forever?', 'Why can't I have a willy?', 'Why were those two men kissing?', 'What's the biggest number in the world?' Their endless stream of enquiries were alternately hilarious, charming, inane, infuriating and rarely easy to answer well. Maybe, I thought, other parents find the whole business easier than me.

Judging by the conversations at the school gates, this wasn't the case. Mothers in particular related their children's questions as an endless source of amusement, sometimes mortification. We sympathised with one another and laugh about those moments, caught in supermarkets or on playdates, confronted with gems such as, 'What's a condom?' and 'Why were you making funny noises in your bedroom last night?' We compared notes. 'What would you have said?', 'What should I have said?' Who really knows?

Despite the wealth of parenting books out there, I couldn't find anything on the subject. How candid, for example, should one be when an inquisitive five year old asks, 'Mum, why did that little girl go missing?' or 'Why can't I trust all strangers?'

Children are constantly learning more about the world, soaking up the media around them and their questions can provoke a conflict. We want to protect them but we also wish to increase their awareness and knowledge – and that means telling the truth. But how much?

While frequently floored by my children's curiosity, I have also been inspired by it and I really did want to find out the definitive answer to certain questions; why a zebra has stripes and how language first came about, for example. Children, it seems to me, ask far more penetrating and perceptive questions than many adults. They're certainly prepared to challenge aspects of our culture that grown-ups have become inured to. 'Why is that man sleeping on the street?', for example, and 'Why does Daddy never use the washing machine?' I'd still like to know the answer to that one.

Which is why *Ask Your Father*, originally a column in *The Times*, came into being. As my column became more established, I received hundreds of questions from children all over the country. The final selection, I hope, offers a realistic snapshot of what really concerns, baffles, fascinates and perplexes a broad range of children – from three year olds to adolescents. I wanted to give them the answers they deserved – and that meant approaching the experts.

These answers would be nowhere near as instructive, illuminating and as authoritative as they are without the generous input from the country's leading child psychologists, psychotherapists, philosophers, theologians, linguists, political academics and mathematicians.

I found myself in a remarkably privileged and enjoyable

position – not many mothers I know could pick up the phone and ask Marcus du Sautoy, author and professor of mathematics at Oxford University, his advice on what to tell my five year old when he was keen to know what infinity was all about. Or AC Grayling, author and professor of philosophy at Birkbeck College, University of London, what I should advise one perplexed eight year old who wondered, 'If there's a God, why are there so many wars?' Tony Benn was invaluable, I hope, in mobilising one apathetic female teen who wrote in to ask, 'Why should I bother voting?' It was a rather less enviable task calling one of the country's leading biological anthropologists, Dr Christophe Soligo, to ask him his thoughts on one five year old's enquiry, 'Mummy, what's that fur between your legs?' Or Tony McEnery, professor of linguistics at Lancaster University for a detailed explanation on the etymological derivation of 'wanker', which he charmingly and patiently gave me.

Which brings me to a central aim of *Ask Your Father* – to treat every child's question with equal gravity, respect and attention, regardless of its apparent crudity or embarrassment potential. Among the child psychologists I consulted, all were unanimous that children should be able to feel they can ask their parents anything they wish; that nothing is off limits.

They were also clear that if you want your child to carry on asking questions – and learning from you – tell the truth. Always. If they ask, 'Have you ever smoked?', and you have, don't feel you have to conceal it completely. It is a valuable lesson for them to learn that adults are fallible and everyone can make mistakes. Once you're aware of that, answering questions becomes a lot more relaxed. Not that we should give away too much detail – always explain as much as you feel you can without fuelling unnecessary anxiety is the general message.

Many psychologists and therapists I spoke to agreed that children are so adept at picking up on what's going around them, their questions should encourage us to reflect more on our own beliefs and attitudes, and to be aware of how profoundly our relationships effect their well-being. Which is why I've included more personal questions like, 'Dad is the boss isn't he?' and 'Why were you shouting at each other last night?'

Above all, being a curious parent is the best way to foster curiosity in our own children. If we're attentive, interested and stimulated, always questioning what we see around us, our children will be more likely to model that behaviour too.

In past generations it was broadly acceptable to dismiss their inquisitiveness with a, 'Go ask your father, dear'. But not now – because we're beginning to understand the crucial role that curiosity plays. It is a way of enriching our relationships, hopefully way into adolescence and beyond, so we know what excites, worries and frightens our children. The more in tune we are with our children's questions, the more they will continue to learn, discover and take pleasure in the world around them.

THE ONES YOU WISH THEY'D NEVER ASK...

'Mummy, why were you and Dad making funny noises last night?'
Laura, 7

'Er, Daddy and Mummy were just fooling around. We didn't realise we'd woken you up, darling', is an explanation most parents don't look forward to uttering when they've just been caught in flagrante.

As well as embarrassment at the thought of discovering a small person at the end of the bed silently witnessing our most intimate of moments, there is anxiety. We worry that what our child glimpses will disturb and upset them. 'It could be that it taps into our anxieties about sexual behaviour – there's still this idea that sex is a bit corrupting if someone else sees it. We're allowed to do it but behind closed doors, it's somehow sinful', says Petra Boynton, sex and relationship psychologist specialising in sex education. 'It's only in recent times we've grown so prudish.' As Boynton points out, 'Within the last century, children would have lived in overcrowded conditions and almost certainly overheard sex. It wasn't viewed with the same anxiety.'

Experts agree that there is nothing harmful about children seeing parents' sexual behaviour. Parents are more likely to react badly, not their children. 'They're the ones who are embarrassed but the children generally take it in their stride', says Paula Hall, sexual psychotherapist for Relate.

Boynton agrees. 'The key issue isn't them seeing you having sex but how you deal with it afterwards. What doesn't work is to deny anything was going on; then they'll think, 'Who was making those noises?' or 'Why are Mummy and Daddy being so secretive?'

Instead, an open and lighthearted response is probably the best one. 'You could say something like, "We were just having fun and cuddling together; that's what Mummys and Daddys do sometimes", says Hall. What they're interested in is the noise, not the sexual activity itself, so it's key to reassure them that neither Mummy or Daddy has been hurt or upset by the activity. 'If they seem concerned, you could say, "Did it worry you?" it's fine to ask this and can open up the conversation', says Boynton. Or they may simply be curious – if so, you don't have to go into too much detail. Boynton adds, 'Be very matter of fact. It can be light-hearted with laughing, so they know that there's nothing to worry about. It's good if they can pick up that it's a nice thing; something you feel relaxed about that isn't scary or forbidden.'

If you don't want it to happen again (the interruptions, not the sex), maybe you should take some precautions. 'You may want to change your bedroom arrangements, move the bed against another wall if it's close to your child's bedroom wall. You can do particular things like turn some music on too. These measures are about tact and sensitivity rather than secrecy', says Hall. As she says, 'It never affects anyone adversely. If anything it's positive that you're modelling healthy sexuality in a loving relationship. They know Mum and Dad are enjoying some private time "playing" and that's positive in itself.'

Unless, of course, you get the question, 'But why can't I play too?'

'Mummy, why don't you have a willy?'
Thomas, 4

There's no possibility of evasion here – nothing but a direct answer will suffice. Be prepared to give them enough facts without telling them more than they need to know. At 4 years old, a detailed anatomical roadmap of the female genitalia won't mean much to them – but don't shy away from the essential details.

'What they need at this age isn't particularly graphic or explicit', agrees relationship expert Christine Webber. 'I think you should say, "Dads, or men, have willies and they need them to wee from. Mums, or girls, don't have them because we don't need them. We have another hole to wee from." Very often that is quite sufficient. At this stage, it's not a sexual issue but a case of just noting the differences.'

But is it? There are other issues at stake here. You may want to take steps to frame what girls supposedly don't have in a more positive way; what you don't want to infer is that young Thomas has a willy and by contrast poor Mummy has a physical absence. Petra Boynton, sex and relationship psychologist says, 'I would avoid this by starting with what Mummy has and then going onto what Daddy has. If you say Mummy doesn't have one it could make the child think that Mum *should* have one, subtly implying that having a penis is better.'

That sense of phallic superiority is evident from such a young age – I have yet to hear about a 4-year-old girl asking her father why he hasn't got a vulva. Yet it is also easy to understand, historically rooted as it is in our language – just look at the wealth of available terms to describe 'willy' and the marked absence of appropriate words that refer to female genitalia. A minefield, you will rapidly discover, when it comes to telling young Thomas what you – and his sister – have got instead of a penis.

Clearly you need to use a name you feel truly at ease with. 'If you go silly or twee or disrespectful your children will pick up on any emotional ambivalence in your tone. You really need to think about it beforehand', advises Kairen Cullen, child psychologist. 'I wouldn't dictate the language you should use because it is so personal – it's to do with our own comfort levels.'

Webber and Boynton tentatively suggest using vulva, which sounds very grown up and could possibly be confused with something Swedish and sensible that Mummy drives. The delicate issue of the naming of parts is something that's good to resolve as early as possible – think of suitable names and stick to them.

Finally, thanking your child for asking such a question is probably the last thing on your mind but Boynton recommends it. 'Saying something like, "Thank you for asking that. It's an interesting question...", is giving a message to the child that it's perfectly ok to talk around this topic. Even if you find it embarrassing, try to give them a straightforward answer because it makes them feel so much more comfortable.'

'Mummy, why does fiddling with myself feel so nice?' Bruno, 5

Masturbation is still one of the most taboo areas of sexual activity and no-one really knows why. 'It's the big issue that never gets talked about in society and families', says Christina Fraser, relationships counsellor and psychotherapist. 'We learn to box it up and deal with it alone. What children do is bring openness and innocence to it and parents can find that difficult to cope with. I suspect the majority of couples don't talk about it and that gets projected onto the child.'

There are two key points to convey to Bruno – firstly that masturbation is a perfectly healthy aspect of sexual development. Secondly, even though there should be no shame attached, it is a private activity.

'What you've got to get across is that it is a nice feeling, there's nothing wrong with that. Give them positive reinforcement about it. But there's also a time and a place', says Sarah Fletcher, psychosexual therapist. In other words, not in the sitting room when granny has come to tea.

'It can create a lot of anxiety in parents', says Fletcher. 'It can also be particularly embarrassing in younger children – often parents will talk about their two or three-year-old daughters gleefully rubbing themselves for all the world to see. Parents can feel extremely uncomfortable when small children do it in public – especially as we often don't remember having any sexual feelings when we were that young. What I say to them is it's completely normal. We have to encourage children to know it's ok – at certain times when they're on their own.'

Bodily exploration is part of normal development and can often begin at around two years old, when they first move out of nappies into pants and suddenly discover they've got access. Girls are easily as curious as boys at this stage, deriving just as much pleasure, which can also cause parental discomfort. 'I suspect this is because we somehow feel boys can't control themselves but girls should be able to, so we deal with it diffferently.' says Fraser.

Even though it isn't sexual at this age, it is definitely pleasurable, in the same way that it is for adults. At two or three years old, when they have no real concept of privacy, you can simply ignore the behaviour or gently distract them – often they'll do it simply because they can. Rather like picking their nose, it can simply be because they've got nothing better to do and their hands are free.

When they reach five years old, keep your explanation simple. 'That feels nice', you can reassure them. 'But maybe not now, and not in front of other people.' Above all, be watchful of your own reactions and aware that how you respond can have an enormous influence. As Fraser says, 'What you're giving a child is their earliest experiences of how to deal with sexual feelings – and it has everything to do with your own attitude. You want to avoid attaching what they do to any sense of shame.'

There certainly shouldn't be any – as Woody Allen once said, 'Don't knock masturbation; it's sex with someone I love.'

'Mummy, what's that fur between your legs?'
Chloe, 5

An unflattering observation that makes poor Mummy sound as if she's barely evolved from the primates, let alone graced a salon for a bikini wax in the last two years. At least you can console yourself that Chloe didn't call it a beard.

What you can point out to her is that human beings don't have fur, not even Mummy, but they do have pubic hair – a particular type of coarse hair that begins to sprout when we reach a certain age called puberty. That is probably all that five-year-old Chloe needs or wants to know as far as sexual development is concerned.

Her question can, once you've stepped out of the shower or bath and regained a little dignity, prompt an interesting discussion about hair and human evolution. You could ask Chloe why does she think we have hair where we do? And why we don't have it all over our bodies like say, cats or dogs, rather than in a few isolated patches?

Let her explore some possibilities before you explain, with admirable anthropological understanding, that what sets humans apart from most other mammals is our nakedness not our hairiness. You can add that although we do still possess hair over our bodies, it has become so flimsy it is barely visible. The reason for this could be because we evolved as a running animal – to hunt efficiently as well as to flee other predators. 'Men can run down deer and horses if they want to. We're pretty good at it', says Jack Cohen, reproductive biologist and honorary mathematics professor at the University of Warwick. 'But we need to get rid of a lot of heat while we're running – our heart rate can increase more than four times its normal level – and we sweat more efficiently when we don't have hair.'

Any remaining hair is there for good reason, you can tell Chloe. Hair on the head helps to protect us from the elements – wind and rain as well sun. You could also say it's there to distinguish the sexes; hair allows women and men to look extremely different, which in turn makes them more attractive to one another. Eyebrows still survive because they can protect our eyes from sweat. Which leaves armpits and, er, that fur between the legs again.

So why do we still have it? The age at which we grow pubic hair is the first indication of what it's related to – sexual development and maturity. Crucially, though, it's all down to smell, says Dr Christophe Soligo, biological anthropologist at University College London. 'We have two types of sweat glands. One is eccrine and the other is apocrine, which you only get under the arms and in the pubic area. Apocrine glands secrete a viscous fluid which helps to generate an individual body odour.'

In experiments, says Soligo, women have literally sniffed out, from a selection of body odours, men who differ most from themselves in terms of genetic make-up – so reducing the risk of in-breeding. All this information is contained, incredibly, in the musky scent of underarm and pubic hair, says Soligo. Not that you'll be able to explain much of this to Chloe – it's probably more advisable to cease the discussion soon after the eyebrows. To avoid anymore taxing questions in this area, book a Brazilian now.

'Mummy, what's a period?'
Esme, 6

We all know the answer to this question but the dilemma is, at such a young age, how much information to give? Instinctively, most of us probably feel that a graphic description of the menstrual cycle isn't quite appropriate. Equally, one doesn't want to brush away what is a crucial aspect of female health, and one that Esme has every right to know about. So what is the sensible middle ground?

'I would say let the child run the agenda on what they want to know', says Christine Webber, relationship expert. 'Keep it brief, give a proper answer but then don't elaborate – unless they want to know more. Five to six years old is not the right time for an explanation about the role of sperm and eggs,' she says. 'Around nine to ten years old is a better time.' Instead you could tell young Esme, 'Once a month grown up women have a small blood loss and we wear something called a tampon or a pad to make sure it doesn't go on our clothes.' And leave it at that.

Of course Esme could look worried and ask if everyone has them. 'In which case', advises Webber, 'You can say, "All grown-up women have them and so will you when you're a big girl." They might ask if it hurts and you should say, "no, it doesn't". You may have to lie here if you do get severe period pain; I don't think it's necessarily a good thing to lay that on your six year old.'

Understandably there is still the underlying fear of upsetting children with the mere mention of blood. As Dr Carol Cooper, family doctor and co-author of *Your Child Year By*

Year, says, 'It can be daunting for children to be told too much, especially when blood is involved and they associate that with pain. The idea of giving it piecemeal can be more comfortable for parents. Taking a deep breath and spilling all the beans doesn't always work.'

Historically, it's not a subject we've ever felt comfortable discussing, which doesn't make Esme's question any easier to answer. As Janice Delaney, Mary Lupton and Emily Toth write in their book, *The Curse, A Cultural History of Menstruation*, 'Greater than his fear of death, dishonour, or dismemberment has been primitive man's respect for menstrual blood.' This taboo element still lurks to some extent. But any reluctance or anxiety to discuss it is something children will tune in to immediately, so be aware of your own feelings on the subject – whether you find the topic embarrassing – and try to be as relaxed and open as possible. Reassure yourself that your child will set their own limits. As Dr Cooper says, 'I know one mother who tried to tell her young daughter and she put her hands over her ears, insisting, "Stop Mum. I'm not ready for this."' At which point you can very happily change the subject and talk about something else instead.

'Mummy, why do your bosoms look so empty?' Maisie, 6

No aspect of the ageing process can be hidden from the searing gaze of a young daughter, and a sagging decolletage is no exception.

Brutally will she expose every blemish, fault, wrinkle and droop. Get used to it because as the years roll by there'll be worse to come; 'Why are you wearing *that* at your age?' 'Why do the backs of your legs look like orange peel?' 'Why does that mole on your face look like a squashed fly?'

Still, what you don't want to convey is any lurking bitterness or loss of self-esteem linked with how you feel about your physical appearance. It is entirely normal for us to mourn, usually in brightly-lit changing rooms, a certain youthful elasticity that passed with our first and subsequent pregnancies. But it's not something we should really expose our children to.

Try not to make it personal even if you do feel that way, as in, 'Breast-feeding you for six months may have had something to do with it.' Remain equable and factual. Explain that every woman has different sized breasts depending on their build.

It may help – and reassure you – to know why some breasts will always look different to others. 'They are composed of different amounts of two components', explains Dr Joanna Scurr, a lecturer in sport and exercise science at the University of Portsmouth who has researched breast health. 'The glandular tissue consisting mainly of the milk reservoir and the fat that lies on top of that. You can get different percentages depending on your level of body fat.'

You can also explain that the shape of our breasts alter throughout our lives, from puberty onwards and particularly during and after pregnancy. 'They increase in density and firmness when the milk reservoir fills up. Then they get less firm when milk is no longer stored because the supporting structure of the breast is stretched and doesn't shrink back', says Scurr. 'But small breasts can do their work just as well as bigger ones and from a sporting perspective, it can certainly give you an advantage.'

This can lead onto a more general discussion about relative physical merits. 'You can explain that everyone is different; some of us have long fingers or long legs but the really important thing is what people are like; whether they are kind and nice,' says Christine Webber, relationship expert. 'Pay careful attention to your feelings too,' she adds, 'if the question comes from your daughter. If you have any body issues these can drip down to small children without you realising it.' So let her know that Mummy is content, thanks to the miracles of modern lingerie, with her cleavage even if it isn't quite as defined as it once was.

As ever, a resilient, iron-coated ego helps, along with a breezy acceptance to try and make the best of what you possess. 'They're not what they once were', you could agree. 'But it's nothing that a Wonderbra can't sort out, dear.'

'Mummy, what's a condom?'
Alice, 6

So you're getting dressed and Alice is rifling through Daddy's bedroom drawer, and swoops like a magpie on a shiny foil packet. Why couldn't she alight on Daddy's hair trimmer instead, you wonder. Typically it's you, not him, who is left to explain the glories of the condom.

You can reassure yourself that it could have been a lot worse. You could be on the Pill in which case Alice's discovery would have been an emotional bombshell, rather than an embarrassing blip. 'It does happen more than you'd think,' says Dr Petra Boynton, sex and relationships psychologist. 'Depending on how you handle the situation, children can grow up feeling very guilty about sex, if they feel their discovery has had serious consequences.'

Assuming it isn't a nasty surprise for you, then Alice's curiosity should prompt a simple, truthful answer, one which doesn't have to involve any detailed explanation. 'Since this is really a question about sex and relationships, we tend to feel guilty that somehow it has to become an impromptu sex lecture. It doesn't,' says Boynton. It's perfectly acceptable to answer in the same way you would were Alice to stumble across, well, Daddy's ear-hair trimmer; as in, "Oh that's just something that belongs to Daddy. Can you put it back where you found it?"'

'A very short answer is fine at this age and more than likely they'll go away happy,' adds Boynton. 'Although what you don't want to do is make them feel naughty or awkward for asking about it.' Your job is to be matter of fact, rather than embarrassed or dismissive. It's one thing telling them what a condom is but what if Alice wants to see it? 'This is a dilemma,' agrees Boynton. 'Some parents may feel fine getting one out and showing it to them. At that age, they would think it was funny and try playing with it like a balloon. Others would feel happier saying, "I'll show you when you're a bit older." It really depends on how relaxed you feel.'

Dr Carol Cooper, family doctor and co-author of *Your Child Year By Year* agrees simplicity is key. 'I would advise answering in a way that doesn't give more than you have to,' she says. 'Depending on how much your child knows then there's no harm in explaining that a condom stops the seed reaching the egg. But really they've got to know about why adults have sex other than procreation, which is quite a big leap.'

When Cooper's five-year-old son discovered a condom and asked the million dollar question, Cooper managed to impart enough, without telling too much. 'I said, "It's something men sometimes use on their willies to stop infection" and made it clear it was for adult men. He wasn't really interested anymore after that.' It didn't take him long to catch up. 'Two years later, I found myself telling them off and saying, "Why have I got three such naughty boys?" and he replied, "Well, Mum, you should have used a condom."'

'Mummy, our teacher says we've got sex education next week, what's that?'
Mia, 7

Sex education is a hot term at the moment. No doubt Mia will have heard it thrown around on television or radio, or she's seen one of the recent leaflets *Let's Grow with Nisha and Joe*, aimed at younger primary school children. Some parents are concerned that an educational pamphlet spelling out a few body parts will corrupt their young children's minds. Others feel it doesn't go far enough, citing research that shows the more our children know about sex, the less promiscuous they grow up to be. Where you lie on the spectrum will, inevitably, influence your answer.

You may feel uncomfortable talking about sex education and what it entails, or feel that you should be ready with the facts immediately, fearing that otherwise the window of opportunity will close. 'I would say you do know a lot more than you think', says Petra Boynton, sex and relationship psychologist. 'If your child came home with a maths problem and you said you didn't know how to do it, you wouldn't view yourself as a failure. So approach this in the same way. You can say, "I'm not sure what this is about – let's find out together."'

Your first response could be to ask Mia what she thinks sex education means. 'Sometimes they have an idea and you can proceed from there,' says relationships expert Christine Webber. 'They may have got it slightly wrong but it will give them the chance to build on what they know.'

You could clarify with a simple explanation like, 'It's all to do with grown up people loving each other and how they can have babies if they want to.' 'Keep it anatomical and baby focussed,' says Webber, 'rather than getting into the area of how it's a pleasurable activity, which at six or seven years old you don't really have to go into so much.' Boynton agrees, 'If you start by saying, "It's all about where babies come from", you'll end up having to have that conversation. A reasonable way in is to say, "It's about living with someone, having boyfriends and girlfriends and being in love."'

Which is, for many of us, an easier place to begin than an anatomical lecture on fallopian tubes. Even the term sex education can sound much too dry and formal. 'I wish they'd change the name', says Boynton. Since we're stuck with something that sounds distinctly 1950s, it is worth emphasising that sex education embraces all aspects of relationships and is something that can be discussed at home, anytime, as well as in school. 'The best way to tackle the subject is to answer children's questions as and when they come up', says Webber, 'rather than assuming it's the school's responsibility. View it as part of a shared and pro-active discussion and make sure you're not like one mother who told her child, "Sex education? That's something you learn at home, not at school, and that's the last I'll say on the subject."'

'Mummy, have you or Dad ever taken drugs?'
Jamie, 11

For those among us who have never smoked or ingested anything more mind-altering than an aspirin, this question will present no moral or personal dilemma whatsoever. You may as well look away now. For the sizeable minority of parents still remaining, dread lurks at how best to tackle this one. Instinct impels us not to reveal the whole truth, as in, 'Yes, darling, I was stoned when I first met your father otherwise I'd never have been remotely interested.' Evasion, along the lines of, 'Well, dear, it depends on how you define drugs. Alcohol is a drug, and so is Calpol – so you could say we've both taken drugs', feels a little cowardly and, besides, our children just wouldn't buy it. Then there's condemnation, 'All drugs are bad. Our behaviour is beyond reproach and we expect yours to be too', which you worry would drive your children in the opposite direction.

Most experts would point us towards a mixture of elements from the first two options. Yes, be honest, but guardedly so. If questions become too probing, some evasion isn't a bad thing, and don't be afraid to present yourself as a realistic example. 'I did experiment as a young person but what I learnt is it was not for me.' Experts agree that telling as much as you can bear to without making either you or your child feel uncomfortable is the best policy. 'Be honest but not preposterously so,' advises Professor Richard Hammersley, a health psychologist and addiction expert at Glasgow Caledonian University. 'Completely lying is a mistake. I think the question needs to be taken in context of substance use in general. Most people in the UK drink, a large number still smoke cigarettes and a similar size have tried cannabis. I don't see why there shouldn't be a reasonably open discussion about that. My children know I used to smoke cigarettes but also that I gave up because it was bad for my health.'

How much you disclose is a highly personal decision but it is also key both in shaping your child's values and being credible in their eyes, so they trust your opinion in future. It's one thing to say you've tried them; what about admitting they can actually be enjoyable? 'One of the big issues here is accuracy,' says clinical psychologist and parenting expert Claire Halsey. 'The draw of drugs is that initially they can make you feel good. If you just talk about the negative aspects, they'll soon find out from their friends and think you're exaggerating. So don't try and hide the fact that the initial feeling can be pleasant but do talk about the downsides; how it can affect your mood and your health.' The best approach is preparation; if you don't want to squirm over your cornflakes when this one pops up, think in advance about what you feel you can tell them. As Hammersley says, 'It's not about answering one question but having an on-going discussion; building slowly as they become more ready to listen.'

'Mummy, why are those two men kissing?'
Grant, 8

Rather than fretting how far this question will take you into unchartered territory, reassure yourself instead that it is actually a timely way of gauging your child's awareness of sexual matters. By eight or nine years old, you'll have a pretty good idea of how much your child knows about relationships through the type and variety of questions that they are asking. 'As a parent you should really welcome this kind of query,' agrees child psychologist Kairen Cullen. 'It's a window into understanding where your child is developmentally and you can use that as a basis for other conversations. Talking about different types of sexual relationships should be part of an on-going conversation, a continuum where you can help them to see the bigger picture at their

pace, over weeks, months and years.'

In this case, the bigger picture doesn't have to be that detailed: don't feel you have to dive in at the deep end. Start off shallow, and see how it goes. 'The best way is to simply say, "This is what couples do when they like each other and want to show affection, like Mummy and Daddy do,"' says Paula Hall, relationship therapist for Relate. 'Then you can say that sometimes a couple can be two men, or two women.' Your child may respond with a more leading question, or not. 'If the conversation ends there, then that's enough,' says Hall. Keep it simple and don't feel you have to introduce too much information. 'I'm a firm believer that children ask questions they're ready to hear the answers for.'

The next logical question could be, 'Can they have babies?' 'You'll need to explain that only women can have babies but it's a good opportunity to explain that, even so, everyone can be parents; men can adopt and so can women,' says Hall. Families with one Mummy and one Daddy can seem like the norm but there are many different alternatives that work as well, you could say.

Always take your cues from your child's response, says Gaynor Sbuttoni, educational psychologist. 'You do have to get the measure of your child. Depending on how they ask the question, you can say, "That sounds like it's confusing you". In this way, you can read back how they're feeling to help them make sense of the issue.'

An inquisitive eight year old may well ask why or how two men can be a couple? In which case, you have to explain that fancying or liking other people is all a matter of taste. 'Use examples that they'll understand', says Hall. 'Like, some people love ice cream and chocolate, others like different sorts of food. Just like food, we're attracted to different sorts of people; some of us like tall people, others like blondes. We're all different.' Thank goodness for that, you could justifiably add.

'Mummy, why have you always got a glass in your hand?' Euan, 7

'Well, Euan, it tastes really nice and, er, I find it helps me to relax and make my evening more enjoyable,' is one response. The question is, how honest should we be?

In my household, both my children have grown rather too used to their parents' fondness for an after-work tipple. Like many parents, as our children grow older and observe our habits, we feel a mix of unease and anxiety. How much are our children imprinting; will our drinking habits create a future generation of heavier drinkers? How should we respond to our children's natural curiosity?

'It is best to be honest,' advises Richard Hammersley, a professor in health psychology at Glasgow Caledonian University. 'You could say something like, "I enjoy the taste but, unfortunately, it can be bad for you." It's a tricky issue but if you tell them drinking is wicked and terrible, when they get older and discover it isn't, your credibility as a source of information will be blown.' Talking openly about alcohol is, says Hammersley, the way forward. 'You should be able to have discussions, when they're slightly older, about the unfortunate affects and even to say, "Yes, it has been known for Mum and Dad to drink too much the odd time". Use it as a learning experience rather than lying.'

While you're at it, you could also be pedantic with Euan

about his use of 'always', assuming you're not staggering around the house glass-in-hand throughout the day. As child development psychologist Elaine Douglas says, 'Children can exaggerate and you could say, "I don't always have a glass in my hand. It's occasional or at mealtimes with friends etc." Also I wouldn't enter into an answer in great depth.' Douglas counsels brevity instead. 'I would say I do enjoy the taste, just like they like the taste of Ribena and really try to leave it at that.' What's more important than the answer, says Douglas, is being honest with yourself in the first place. 'You do need to exercise some insight and self-awareness,' says Douglas. 'Children do copy and mimic and you are a role model for your child; if every single day you're wandering around with a glass in your hand, you have to ask what messages you are giving to your child.'

In other words, if you're worried about how to answer Euan, then maybe it's better to think about altering your drinking patterns before he's old enough to ask. As Hammersley says, 'If you think that your drinking levels can't stand up to your child looking at them, then that's a sign it's too much. If you don't want your child to see, then you need to ask yourself some questions.'

Although let's not be too hasty; giving up drinking isn't the best option either. For the simple reason – and we can all draw a collective sigh of relief here – that when the drinking habits of America's Bible Belt were researched, the results turned out to be very polarised: either people tended to drink heavily or not at all. It is a similar pattern in the western Highlands, where one fifth of the population abstain and a third drink more than average. So, one can only conclude that drinking small, sensible amounts in front of our children can be viewed as a social responsibility; an acceptable rather than a guilty pleasure. 'It is better to give children a model of moderate positive social drinking,' agrees Hammersley. We can all raise a glass to that.

'Mummy, what's a wanker?'
Johnny, 6

Try, if you can, to suppress any initial shock or embarrassment, even if Johnny does choose to raise this query in a queue of Tesco shoppers – all keen, no doubt, to hear your colourful explanations of onanism. At that moment, you're perfectly entitled to duck the issue with a, 'That's an interesting question, Johnny, let's talk about it more when we get home'.

When you do answer him, and you certainly should, be positive that he has come to you for an explanation. Then remind him that there are some words it is fine to ask about but not acceptable to employ in daily language. Wanker is evidently one of them. 'Children should feel they're able to ask the meaning of anything but then the parent has to emphasise the distinction between understanding a term and actually using it,' says Tony McEnery, professor of linguistics at Lancaster University and author of *Swearing in English. Bad Language, Purity and Power from 1586 to the Present*.

It may be interesting for you to know that wanker is a relative newcomer in the illustrious history of British swear words. Originating from British and Australian slang of the 1940s, its literal meaning (one who masturbates) rapidly became a more generic insult; aimed usually at males and associated with someone who is egotistical and self-obsessed. More recently, pretentiousness and snobbishness have been added to the list of contemptible traits that the term embraces.

Of course, giving Johnny this level of detail would be entirely unsuitable, as Dr Rachel Andrew, a child psychologist who specialises in family issues, says, 'All you need say is that it's not a word we like to use but that it means idiot, and people sometimes shout it when they're cross with someone. Keep it minimal and don't make too much fuss or give it too much attention.'

Although don't give it so little attention that Johnny has no sense of what it could possibly mean. 'There is a general problem that children can hear words they sense are taboo and if they don't find out the accurate meaning, they may say it and people will think badly of them,' says McEnery. Reassure yourself that your child is inquisitive, values and trusts your relationship enough to to ask you and, crucially, that you could be saving him from years of future misunderstanding and embarrassment.

Look no further, says McEnery, than the rather unexpected example of Victorian poet Robert Browning. 'He never asked anyone what the word "twat" meant and in his poem *Pippa Passes*, he rhymes it with bat.' Disastrously he assumed it was an item of clothing, headwear for nuns to be precise, and no-one, including his mother, presumed to put him straight.

This should serve as a cautionary tale for one mother whose six-year-old son turned to her during a particularly profane football match and asked her what a wanker was, since the man behind him was shouting it so liberally. She thought for a moment, 'Well Josh, it's just another name we call the referee.'

WHAT ON EARTH...

'Mummy, why do zebras have stripes?'
Finn, 9

Because they'd look silly with polka dots? More sensibly you could inform Finn that he's alighted on an evolutionary conundrum that has preoccupied scientists for centuries. The number of conflicting theories out there – and there are several – is evidence of how undecided the experts still are. You could start by telling Finn that zebra stripes are rather like human fingerprints – no two are ever the same. Then you could ask him why he thinks they have stripes at all. He will probably mention camouflage – the most obvious answer – until you reflect what a poor imitation of camouflage it really is. As Dr Graham Hemson, zoologist at Oxford University's wildlife conservation unit says, 'Very few people who see zebras out in the savannah will say, "Gosh, that's very well camouflaged."' Even elephants are harder to spot in their natural habitat. Not that Finn is wrong exactly – the definition of camouflage in its broader sense can mean simply confusing predators, and this begins to make more sense.

The theory is that the pattern of a zebra's hide is more crucial than the colour because lions, a zebra's main predator, are colour-blind. Another view is that their markings allow zebras to blend in with one another, so a lion is unsure what to charge at. 'The stripes confuse predators,' says Tom Lowry, keeper of mammals at London Zoo. 'Black and white may not be common colours on the savannah but that doesn't matter. It breaks up the outline of the individuals and makes each separate animal much more difficult to spot.' So it is difficult to see where one zebra begins and another ends, particularly useful for protecting the weaker, more vulnerable members of the herd. Or as Hemson puts it, 'If you're the lion, it's like attacking a huge moving barcode'.

This is also a highly credible theory when it comes to the zebra's offspring, he adds. 'You could argue that zebra foals have long legs that are disproportionate to their bodies. Why? So they are elevated to the same level as their parents; with their stripy colouration they too blend in with the adults.' A more recent theory, says Hemson, is related to the tzetze fly. 'These flies carry sleeping sickness, a parasitic disease that is a major cause of disease among ungulates (hooved animals). But it's been found that they're less likely to land on a striped background than a uniformly-coloured one.' Let's hope Finn doesn't ask how on earth they managed to work that one out.

Which leads onto why this whole question is so fearsomely tricky to answer. 'Unless you got a whole bunch of donkeys and zebras and drove them across the Serengeti to see which is more likely to survive, it would be very difficult to test out. It's never really been important enough to discover; it's not a conservation issue as such, more of a scientific curiosity.' Hemson has his own theory. 'A nice one is that the stripes act as a cooling mechanism; they heat up at different rates because black absorbs heat and white reflects it. So it creates swirling vortices of air currents that cool off the zebra in hot sun.' Now that joke about polka dots doesn't seem so silly after all.

'Mummy, why can't I be King?'
Louis, 5

Would a boy called Dave ask a question like this? I don't think so. If you will call your son Louis, a sense of royal entitlement is likely to run in his blood, even if it's red and not blue. What's important is not to quash his high hopes early on in life. Don't dismiss the notion out of hand, advises Andrew Roberts, British historian and biographer. 'He shouldn't entirely write off his ambitions for the top job. There are few things in Britain that aren't open to meritocracy which is one of the things that makes it such an unusual and interesting country. He could overthrow the government like Oliver Cromwell, who could have been King if he'd wanted it. But, yes', he admits, 'it would take significant constitutional upheaval for him.' Marrying into the royal family would be a less disruptive strategy. 'It wouldn't make him King but it means his eldest son could be.' In other words, a virtually impossible task lies ahead. 'Well, I think Chief Rabbi could be more difficult,' says Roberts.

Without wanting to dishearten any child, including Louis, the realistic answer to his question is 'no, you can't become king' because in Britain we choose our monarchy by blood descent. 'The person who becomes King is the senior heir of the previous one,' explains Anthony Adolph, genealogist and author of Collins' *Tracing Your Family History*. 'It's the system we've had for 1,500 years and it's worked well, give or take the War of the Roses when they were killing off heirs left, right and centre. Louis has inherited his parents DNA and if neither of his parents are royal, then he has inherited no right to the throne.' Something, you can tell him, he can justly blame his family for.

Still, there is another alternative – and suggesting it to any five year old is optional. 'He could kill off everyone between himself and the throne,' says Adolph. 'He would have to trace his family tree and try to find a royal ancestor – which statistically isn't that unlikely; the population in Britain wasn't that big five hundred years ago. Then he would have to murder at least 10,000 people to stand a chance.'

Failing that, he could hope to be a monarch somewhere more hospitable – less fussy – than Britain. There are still plenty around. Currently 44 nations in the world have monarchs, 16 of which are called 'Commonwealth realms', in that they recognise our Queen as their head of state. Which could open up the field for any ambitious king-to-be. 'Go to where they want him,' advises Adolph. Which would be the Baltic States; the leaders of Estonia's Royalist Party asked Prince Edward to be their King and Albania once offered the throne to C.B. Fry, the famous cricketer.

Still, like Roberts, Adolph agrees marriage is probably the best route. 'At least he'd be part of the Royal Family which is as good as he could expect. Either that or tone down his aspirations.'

'Mummy, what's the biggest number in the world?' Billy, 6

If you thought that mathematics might offer some straightforward, concrete answers for your child, think again. Such a question takes us straight into the abstract, imponderable terrain of infinity, eternity and beyond – with serious number-crunching involved. 'My first response is that there isn't a largest number – it's infinity. That idea has challenged mathematicians for sometime,' says Marcus du Sautoy, Professor of Mathematics at Oxford University. The German mathematician Georg Cantor first came up with the concept of an infinity of infinities in answer to this question at the end of the 19th century. 'Cantor ended up in a lunatic asylum,' says Sautoy. 'Partly because he was bi-polar but also because the subject is an unsettling business.' But a fascinating one all the same. 'It's exciting,' says Sautoy. 'The thought that there are different infinities out there. There isn't a last number so you have to bite the bullet and try and think about how numbers just keep going on forever.'

Children probably find it a less disturbing area than adults; in fact, it's one they are naturally drawn to as soon as they start counting, and particularly when they compete with one another to come up with the largest number – around the age of six to seven years old. 'Kids in the playground do have an idea that you can count forever. They always try and trump each other by saying infinity, then infinity plus one and so on,' says Simon Singh, author of *Fermat's Last Theorem* and also a professor of mathematics at Oxford.

You could give them fresh ammunition in the playground with, if not the world's largest number, then some pretty gigantic ones. There's Graham's number – a positively wimpy sounding figure that you feel you should comfortably count on one hand. But no, invented by Ronald Graham, it is often described as the largest finite number that has ever been used as a mathematical proof, and it gets a mention in the Guinness World Records. The number is so vast, there is no concise way to actually write it down. Still, it doesn't sound like a weighty rebuff for Billy should he want to outwit a friend who smugly shouts a million trillion plus one.

He would probably do better armed with a googol, which is the digit 1 followed by one hundred zeros – the concept was introduced in 1938 by the mathematician Edward Kasner, although the name was suggested by his nine-year-old nephew Milton Sirotta. Not satisfied with creating a number more vast than the sum of observable atoms in the universe, Kasner topped it with his googolplex – the digit 1 with a googol number of zeros after it. 'It's just mind-boggingly mind-boggling,' admits Singh. 'Very rapidly you get to numbers that our minds can't comprehend.' It could be more fun to ask your child what *they* would call, given the chance, one of the world's largest numbers – surely they could do better than a Graham?

'Mummy, why do we eat lambs?'
Poppy, 6

Poppy, like all children around this age or even younger, has probably just figured out that what is on her plate – possibly languishing in mint sauce and redcurrant jelly – used to be white and fluffy, and gambol in the meadow. You could, like a friend of mine, avoid telling them that meat is in any way related to any of the furry friends who populate DreamWorks and Pixar but, sooner or later, they will find out. And when they do make a link between tea time and that school trip to a twee Surrey farmyard, you'll need to think up some palatable ways to explain mass culling and abattoirs.

'Children are empathetic to animals in the field and pets, and they don't see any distinction between the two, which in some sense is quite true. Both are sentient beings,' says Caroline Chisholm, spokesperson for the Vegetarian Society. 'Children are also very perceptive and it's important to discuss the issues with them – however young they are. Otherwise they could imagine much worse or be confused. Be honest and informative,' she advises. 'Don't go into too much about blood and gore. You can say at certain times of year, the animals are killed and processed as food.'

Then swiftly distract them with a brief foray into history and religion. Start with the lamb as a symbol; just as the heart is a 'symbol' of love, the lamb is often viewed by religious people as the son of God – sacrificed for our sins. You can say that in past centuries, it was considered good luck to see a lamb, particularly at Easter time, since they represent rejuvenation and hope.

'We always eat lamb at Easter because it's about rebirth,' says Kate Colquhoun, author of *Taste: The History of Britain Through Its Cooking*. Even before Easter, there was a pagan ritual – which is where Easter comes from – based on Eostre, the Teutonic goddess of Spring. You could point out that everyone, including children, enjoy ceremonies, whether it's the harvest festival, Christmas or Easter. 'We cling to these rituals, celebrating and marking different times in the year,' says Colquhoun. 'It's also the time when Jesus rose from the dead and lambs are born; it's to do with things growing and being alive.' Or, as Tom Jaine, food historian and editor of the *Oxford Companion To Food* puts it, 'It's a holy conjunction between Jesus and the season.' Yet lamb, which is killed in its first year of life, is only a relatively recent fashion – our Victorian relations much preferred mutton – otherwise known as sheep at the ripe old age of four to seven years old. 'We never used to eat lamb outside the Spring lambing season,' explains Jaine. 'The rest of the time, we were much more interested in keeping them to grow wool.' Now though, beyond religion and ritual, we carry on eating lamb because it tastes so nice. At it's best, it is one of the most tender, sweet and versatile of meats. As long as Poppy doesn't grow too attached to those sheep in *Babe,* she may well agree.

'Mummy, who invented language?'
Daisy, 7

Firstly, congratulate Daisy for posing such an interesting question. Second, don't feel you should know the answer to this one. Even now, linguists the world over still can't agree about exactly how language developed. Opinion is constantly changing; it's as fluid as language itself.

You could start by saying that language wasn't invented by one person but developed within a community or communities. A million years ago, our ancestors were probably talking but their vocabulary would be unrecognisable today. Scholars are still arguing about its origins – did it start in one place or did we all start talking at around the same time because of the way our brains developed? To which your sensible seven year old may well reply, why can't anyone make up their mind?

'Part of the problem is that early spoken language was never preserved,' explains David Messer, professor of child development and learning at Open University. 'Scientists may have studied skeletons for signs that the mouth and tongue was capable of speech – but it doesn't prove that humans were talking at that time.' It's a good opportunity to explain to your child that scientists and scholars don't necessarily have to agree on how or why certain things happened. 'It means there are lots of possibilities,' says Messer.

Dr James Clackson, senior lecturer in classics, specialising in Greek and Latin linguistics, at Cambridge University explains, 'If you believe language evolved in one place, you believe it's Africa between 100,000 to 200,000 years ago and it spread from there.' According to this theory, a group of humans left Africa, introducing language as they migrated to other areas of the world. Another idea is that language developed from hand gestures that early man used in simple communications. 'Nowadays, however, linguists are more likely to believe that part of our brain is programmed for language as soon as we're born,' says Clackson. You could say that scholars believe that language only came about because of a change in our brains, what they call a 'mutation'.

Most likely, it's a combination of these two theories, says Clackson. 'Language is programmed but we still need stimulus from those around us. From studies we know that if children are isolated from other humans and haven't learnt how to construct sentences by the age of nine years old, it's unlikely they ever will.' Which proves, if nothing else, that language is all about community – no-one could have invented it in isolation. 'If it was just one person, it would be no good,' says Messer. Which is possibly the most interesting aspect for a seven year old. 'A child-friendly way to tackle this is to say we all invent language,' suggests Messer. 'Children may assume it's very static but it's not – go back and look at how different Shakespeare is and that's only 500 years ago. We're all adding and changing words.' No wonder language is so tricky to pin down; it's always in the process of change and that's down to all of us, you could say, even seven year olds.

'Mummy, who decides what name to give a hurricane?' Luca, 9

The naming of hurricanes is a serious business these days, you can tell Luca, agreed upon by an international committee. The National Hurricane Center in Florida has been naming tropical storms since 1953, although the task of what to call Atlantic storms, invariably the most notorious ones, has been handed over to the UN-backed World Meteorological Organisation based in Geneva.

You could explain to Luca that in the past, hurricanes were always female. Most probably they were influenced by a popular novel of the day called *Storm* by George R. Stewart – all about a hurricane named Maria. Soon after its publication in 1941, the National Weather Service followed suit . By the 1970s, this practice was viewed as old-fashioned and possibly a little sexist, so in the spirit of equality the National Hurricane Center decided to name one of the most destructive forces in nature after men too.

Dr Jane Strachan, research fellow for the meteorology department at the University of Reading, explains, 'There are 21 names on each list which are in alphabetical order, excluding the letters Q, U, X, Y and Z. This year we're up to Ike which will be followed by Josephine, Kyle, Laura, Marco and so on.' In a stormy year, this would be followed by Nana, Omar, Paloma, Rene, Sally, Teddy, Vicky and Wilfred. 'The lists are recycled every six years, so we'll see these names again in 2014,' says Strachan. It's difficult to imagine a Teddy or a Vicky reeking much damage but then that's probably what they once said about Katrina. Depending on how deadly a hurricane turns out to be, the name is removed indefinitely. 'They put it into retirement out of respect for victims of the storm,' says Strachan. 'You won't see Katrina again now.'

Luca may want to know what happens if it's a particularly stormy year and there are more than 21 hurricanes. 'It does happen,' says Strachan. 'The worst so far was 2005, with a record 27 storms. They had to move on to the names of the letters from the Greek alphabet – alpha, beta, gamma etc.

At which point Luca may rightly ask, are we getting more hurricanes these days? 'The jury's still out on whether there are more of them due to global warming,' says Strachan. 'The important factor is the temperature of the oceans; that's what gives the storm their energy. If sea temperatures are rising, then hurricanes could get more powerful, although that's not conclusive.'

You could reassure Luca that even though we feel there are more hurricanes around each year, this isn't necessarily the case. Population increases near coastlines have drawn more attention to them and means they pose more threat than they once did, regardless of frequency.

Finally you could mention that in Europe the public can name their own version of a hurricane, a windstorm, thanks to 'Adopt-a-Vortex' – a scheme set up six years ago. People name them after loved ones as well as political heroines. In May 2006, there was one called Condoleezza. In Australia, at the turn of the century, they were also keen on naming their hurricanes after politicians. If Luca asks why, you could suggest the two are not unalike; full of hot air with a tendency to go round in circles.

'Mummy, why is that man's skin so brown?'
Alice, 7

Not a question that many parents relish, least of all if it is asked in public. We worry that a child's frank yet innocent observations can sound offensive, and feel sensitive explaining any difference based solely on skin colour. Yet this is something that interests them and they will, naturally enough, want to know why. Your immediate response is crucial – if you appear evasive or flustered, Alice will associate skin colour with an area that is difficult and taboo. Don't 'Shh' them but respond openly and honestly – try and be comfortable with the subject and explain the facts in an objective and scientific way.

You could say that the simple answer is melanin, a pigment that gives skin and hair its natural colour, as well as the iris in our eyes. More melanin is present in darker skin which protects it against the harmful ultraviolet rays from the sun that can cause skin cancer. You can explain that, in general, people with ancestors from tropical regions have darker skins than those who live in cooler climates. 'Originally the reason that you see such variation is down to environment and where you live in relation to the equator, which influences the level of sun exposure and therefore how damaging it is to your skin,' explains Dr Toomas Kivisild, lecturer in human evolutionary genetics at Cambridge University. Some scientists believe that lighter skin offered much stronger chances of survival for those people who first migrated out of Africa thousands of years ago because it can absorb higher levels of bone-strengthening vitamin D from the sun. Now it is more accepted that genes play a powerful role in determining skin colour, although we have yet to pin down which ones are responsible. 'There are about 20 genes that could explain skin colour but it is still unknown which ones they are,' says Kivisild.

Once you're at home, you can follow up Alice's question with a more general discussion about difference and variety. At seven years old, children are becoming more aware of ethnicity and it's a good time to start talking about it. Point out how different we all are in lots of different ways – from our shape and size to the colour of our hair and our eyes. You can touch on prejudice and mention how we should never judge people for these differences. You could say, 'How would you feel if someone teased you because you had blue eyes and not green eyes – how unfair would that feel?' Use this as an opportunity to talk about your family values, says Claire Halsey, psychologist and parenting expert. 'Discuss what you believe in as a family, about being respectful and always viewing people equally.' As Halsey says, 'You need to embrace this as a curiosity question that should be viewed as part of their development, rather than getting nervous about what it may lead to. It's about stressing that each difference brings a richness to our society – but those beliefs need to be spoken about rather than assumed.'

'Mummy, why do girls prefer pink and boys prefer blue?' Lucy, 9

You could start by complimenting your daughter on her tack-sharp curiosity; although we often complain how stereotyped and restrictive pink for girls and blue for boys is, we rarely pause to consider why. We tend to assume it's always been that way – but it hasn't.

According to historians, at the start of the last century blue was as likely to be a little girl's colour and pink, a boy's. Blue was seen as dainty and delicate while pink was thought to be stronger and bolder. One American newspaper in 1914 even advised mothers, 'If you like the colour note on the little one's garments, use pink for the boy and blue for the girl, if you're a follower of convention.' It was only after World War II that the colour preference reversed, becoming more marked in the '50s and '60s as children became a distinct consumer market.

There's no doubt that the world has turned decidedly pink for girls, thanks to the sugar-sweet strangle hold of Barbie and toy marketing in general. Dividing the sexes by colour encourages us to buy more; no hand-me-downs from older brothers or sisters to younger opposite-sex siblings for a start.

Yet many psychologists are convinced that, beyond commercialisation, girls and boys do prefer contrasting colours. 'I think it follows a clear pattern and there's got to be more to it than culture,' says Elizabeth Hartley-Brewer, a child development specialist. 'Even if girls are encouraged to wear pink, you'd expect 50% to reject it, but they don't. In tests boys always pick out darker colours and girls the lighter ones.'

Although blue has always been popular with both sexes, possibly because it was a symbol of good luck. In ancient myth, it was thought to ward off evil and is also associated with the Virgin Mary.

You could also point out that last year they discovered, for the first time, scientific evidence suggesting that girls are born with an affinity for pink colours. When they asked 208 men and women in their early 20s to choose their preferred colour from a series of paired rectangles, females showed a marked preference for reddish colours. Neuroscientist Dr Anya Hurlbert, who led the research, suggests that this may be down to the way our ancestors used to find food; while women foraged for berries, the men were more likely to go out hunting. 'Evolution may have driven females to prefer reddish colours – reddish fruits, healthy, reddish faces. Culture may exploit and compound this natural female preference.'

A little far-fetched as a theory – it is more likely that what really drives children's taste for different colours is a desire for separate identity. As Dr Lance Workman, an evolutionary psychologist, says, 'Once you've chosen for one gender, the other will want to associate with the opposite. From the age of three years old until adolescence, children don't like the opposite sex so they'll seek out whatever's different.' Hartley-Brewer agrees, 'They're using the colours to explore what it means to be male or female. From seven years old onwards, they're also starting to identify more with their friends – and if they're wearing pink, that's the brand image that they'll choose.'

'Mummy, why does it feel more scary at night time?'
Grace, 6

It is not surprising that Grace finds the world rather more scary after dark since our culture relies on this assumption and has done so for many centuries. Where would the power of our most enduring fairytales and folklore be – legions of monsters, witches, ghouls, ghosts and spirits – without the rich and enduring creative potential that night time offers?

You could argue, not in a way that would make much sense to Grace perhaps, that night time is a depository for our irrational fears, a time when our unconscious insecurities are expressed in dreams; when we can sometimes feel at our most vulnerable and alone.

Evolutionary psychologists would say these feelings are rooted in survival instinct inherited from our ancestors; that our brain is still hardwired to view night time as a hostile place that can deprive our senses and put us at much graver risk from attack. Although Emma Citron, a psychologist specialising in childhood development and fears and phobias, says this has little to do with the secure environment of a child's bedroom. 'There is a sense that bad things are more likely to come out in the dark but if you rationalise it, darkness itself is nothing to be scared of in a safe situation.'

Yet undoubtedly we are – according to a Powergen survey carried out in 2003, 98 per cent of parents leave a light on for their children at night. It is something they quickly become reliant upon. Citron's view is that this is an inevitable consequence of how night time is traditionally portrayed in books and films. 'I would answer the question with another, "What makes you think it is more scary at night?" and confront that assumption. Look at their reasons and explore them. I would bear in mind that there is a drip, drip effect of typical night time imagery; ghosts, Dracula, bats etc – that really isn't helpful to children.'

Citron suggests countering these beliefs by offering more realistic and positive images of night time. 'I took my children to the nocturnal section of London Zoo. We looked at the bats there that are incredibly gentle, sweet-looking creatures who eat strawberries. It's a good education and it's part of saying to your children, "Don't accept at face value these images of darkness you see in cartoons like Scooby Doo."'

Another way is to confront the dark with Grace, suggests educational psychologist Lynette Fry. 'One good exercise is to sit in a darkened room, and let your eyes adjust. Then talk about what you can see, all the familiar objects. Play little games like drawing a letter on their hands and asking them to guess it. In this way you can put a positive slant on it.'

Although that doesn't mean you should deny them all those scarier archetypes that inhabit the night – if Grace can enjoy the thrill of the dark side and is asking the question out of curiosity, then good for her. As Dr Bruno Bettelheim, eminent child psychologist, Freudian analyst and author, wrote in his fascinating investigation of fairytales, *The Uses of Enchantment*, 'Parents believe that only pleasant images should be presented to the child. But such one-sided fare nourishes the mind only in a one-sided way and real life is not sunny.'

No amount of visits to London Zoo can obscure this truth.

'Mummy, is Father Christmas real?'
Joel, 6

We don't turn a hair when our children find out their favourite fictional characters – Snow White, Peter Pan, Superman etc – are just that. But Father Christmas is a fantasy figure of a different calibre. We'll do anything not to shatter this particular childhood illusion, particularly if they're as young as Joel. Which is why it feels so cruel to offer a straightforward 'no' in response. Instinctively the truth feels too brutal, so what is the alternative? Tact and diplomatic fudging, according to child psychologist Kairen Cullen. 'Being black and white about it isn't helpful. I would liken him to other fictional characters your child knows and then focus on what Father Christmas is all about – what he stands for rather than who he is – generosity, goodwill etc.'

What if you've got an astute child who would detect a certain vagueness in the reply, particularly a child like Joel who has expressed scepticism at such a young age? Educational psychologist Gaynor Sbuttoni remembers her four year old quizzing her closely one Christmas, 'He said to me, "He can't really sit in a sleigh with reindeer pulling him and that hole in the chimney is much too small for him to fit down really, isn't it, Mum?"' When your child appears to be asking for the truth, how much should we resist?

'I think if they're this direct, whatever their age, you have to give in,' says Sbuttoni. 'I asked my son why he thought he wasn't real and let his own thoughts lead him.' If they lead indisputably towards the truth, there's not much point trying to sustain the fantasy. 'I believe we have to tell the truth when they want it. I said Father Christmas as a single man riding in his sleigh isn't real but the feelings we have are real,' says Sbuttoni. 'We can still enjoy the pleasure and the happiness that the Father Christmas story brings.'

Developmentally, it's unusual for a four year old to challenge the Father Christmas mystique. Towards seven to eight years old is more common for children to explore and challenge the line between fantasy and reality. At the same age, their grasp of the world increases and so, inevitably, they will start to question the logic of an old man abseiling down every child's chimney. Even so, logic is one thing but you should still be mindful of how crucial these fantasy figures are in developing their imagination and creativity. 'These fictional characters are so important in helping them to make sense of their world, as well as for their psychological and cultural well-being. So it's not going to be good to just give them the blank, bare facts,' says Cullen.

Subtlety is also key since your integrity could be on the line too. 'What you don't want is a child to turn round and say, "You lied to me and I trusted you,"' says Sbuttoni. 'Which is why I would emphasise we can all still enjoy Father Christmas and so why not keep the story going?' That and a solemn promise he'll still get a Nintendo Wii from Santa should do the trick.

I WANT THAT

'Mummy, can I have a toy gun like Alfie's?'
Tom, 4

These days letting your little boy play enthusiastically with a plastic gun in the local playground is as morally acceptable as giving him Coca Cola for breakfast or letting him watch *Rambo*. So parents tend to divide into two camps; the steely, self-righteous ones who enforce a blanket ban on all toy weapons and the rest of us who, as soon we give in to the first innocuous water gun, find ourselves vulnerable to all sorts of dilemmas. If we allow them a toy gun in the home, can they then take it to the park, or their best-friend's party? How to explain that one context feels ok, but another doesn't? Or that plastic water guns in pretty primary colours are somehow more acceptable than an unnervingly realistic black plastic Colt from the local toy shop? One friend insists proudly she would never buy her son a pretend gun, even though he has an extensive armory of water pistols - somehow that makes her feel ok. This speaks more of our own fears - of social embarrassment, as well as our young boys' aggression and how we feel when they express it.

As Gaynor Sbuttoni, educational psychologist who special-ises in the emotional needs of young boys, says, 'If you say "no" to this question and withhold guns completely, they will go out and pick up a stick and pretend it's a gun. You can't prevent children from experiencing things that they need to experience. They will find another way.'

Penny Holland, an academic leader in early childhood at London Metropolitan University and author of *We Don't Play with Guns Here: war, weapon and superhero play*, agrees, 'If we lift zero tolerance, gun play can become less crude and part of more extended scenarios,' she explains, giving the example of the child who pretends to be shot, falls to the ground and then jumps up again alive. 'It's a cycle constantly played out and relates to separation anxiety; the idea of the parent leaving, being absent and then returning. Allowing children space to explore these complex themes is important, even if it can make us feel uncomfortable.'

— why can't I play with guns?

'When they ask this kind of question, I think it is essential to get beyond the knee jerk reaction,' continues Holland. 'What's important is dialogue and discussion. Parents who do decide to buy plastic guns shouldn't be made to feel they're doing something wrong, although they have to be able to help their children understand the difference between fantasy and reality.'

So rather than viewing yourself as a weak, indulgent parent, caving in to your son's primitive impulses, reassure yourself that letting him bound around the garden with a cowboy rifle can be the more responsible and mature option. It also means setting boundaries but not being too controlling or judgmental – no easy feat. 'When they're letting off steam with guns, they're practising being angry. Toy guns are a symbol of masculinity and somehow they – and we as parents – need to work these feelings through and make them feel it's safe to do so,' says Sbuttoni.

'Mummy, can I buy the new Eminem album?'
Ross, 12

Homicide, sexual obsession, infanticide – US rapper Eminem doesn't shy away from the darker aspects of human nature. Which is why even the more liberal-leaning parents may feel troubled at the thought of their 12 year old absorbing some of his more florid lyrical language.

Yet these doubts don't justify a simple 'no'. If the material was too graphic *and* poorly executed, it would be easy to dismiss. Not so with Eminem. His hit 'Stan' – about a deranged fan who kills himself and his pregnant girlfriend – is rated by

Rolling Stone as one of the 500 Great Songs Of All Times. (Sample lyric: 'Shut up bitch. I'm trying to talk. Hey Slim, that's my girlfriend screamin' in the trunk but I didn't slit her throat, I just tied her up, see I ain't like you cause if she suffocates she'll suffer more, and then she'll die too.') Not enough to shock Nigella Lawson who chose him for one of her Desert Island Discs; whether her two children Mimi and Bruno get to listen too we don't know.

So how to reconcile Eminem's artistic worth with the worry of what he actually says, and how he says it? 'I'd be inclined to say, "Come on then, sell it to me – why do you think you should be able to listen to something with explicit lyrics that aren't suitable for your age?"' says Dave Spellman, a clinical psychologist working with adolescents. 'These things should prompt a discussion rather than a parental decree. I think there are circumstances where I could be persuaded by a child's argument or make an exception, so it's important to hear what they come up with. You may as well try and understand them and find out what you're actually objecting to.'

In which case you could suggest listening to the album together. If you know his music, you may want to talk about the lyrics; how Eminem, like many writers, adopts various personas and isn't actually endorsing the crimes that he describes. Or maybe you'd like to listen to the album first, so you know what you're objecting to. Don't be afraid to share doubts and concerns and be open to his opinion.

'If you take a stand and don't enter into a discussion, all they learn is that you're in charge, rather than what the issues are here,' says Spellman. Child psychologist Richard Bailie agrees, 'I would always want to find out where the child is coming from and give them a fair hearing, before I lay down a rule.' Try and establish if they want the album simply because all their other friends have bought it too, he advises. 'If you say "no", you're also saying "I want you to be different from your friends" which in their eyes carries the risk of not being liked – a real social anxiety for them as they approach adolescence.' The key to negotiating these types of questions is to give your child a genuine sense that they are being listened to and understood. You could also reassure yourself that if Nigella has survived unscathed then it's highly likely Ross will too.

'Mummy, can we go to a fast food restaurant?' Cameron, 6

Like it or not, fast food is enshrined in our culture. So even before your six year old asks this, you need to consider how you want your child to view the world's fast food chains which are on every street corner. Since these restaurants serve almost 47 million customers daily, your child will, at some point, almost certainly be one of them. What young child could resist – and should nutritionally-aware parents resist too?

Not necessarily. Trying out the fast-food experience with your child once or twice is a good idea, says Tim Lobstein, director of the Child Obesity Programme for the International Obesity Taskforce in London.

'Never say to your child that he can't try it out,' he says. 'If you do, you run the risk of fetishising it, making it all the more exciting.' You could, like Lobstein, say, 'OK then, let's go.' 'I've taken my children and then taken it apart,' he says. 'When you're there you talk through the experience. So the first chip, you could say, is quite nice. Then say the second or third one is greasy.' Pick up any damp bits of lettuce or ketchup-soaked bun and grimace; chew gingerly and say something like, 'Urggh, I'm really not enjoying this so much.' 'Deconstruct it with them,' advises Lobstein. 'You can say, "Yes, it's tasty and it's not going to kill you. But it would if you ate nothing else".

Another tip Lobstein offers is to buy a burger and chips or fried chicken nuggets and let the food cool down before you take it out of the packaging. Hopefully it will look far less appetising than the air-brushed vision of a plumped-up bun and golden chips that you see on the menu. 'Wait a bit – and it doesn't take long – for the hamburger to look greasy, the bun to deflate and the milkshake to collapse into a flat-looking pink liquid. It's also a really good way of learning how they create a product that works immediately, at the moment it's sold, but not for long after. Whereas healthy food tends to look edible even when it's been around for a while,' says Lobstein. All of which you can then explain.

Crucially, don't get into stand-off and let a request prompt a parent-child battle. Remember who you're fighting here. The battle is against the allure of fast-food – and that's the important one to win.

'Mummy, can I watch more telly?'
Craig, 8

A phrase guaranteed to haunt us during holidays and weekends. In some homes I can think of, such a request will come soon after breakfast and repeat itself until an irate mother marches up to the telly, switches it off and demands that her offspring do 'something more constructive than watching this rubbish, like drawing. Remember drawing?' There must be a more effective strategy for curbing their viewing hours, but it is difficult to negotiate when your children have descended into that slack-jawed vegetative state that wall-to-wall *Ben 10*, *Scoobie Doo* and *Sponge Bob Square Pants* can often induce. Psychologists euphemistically refer to this state as attentional inertia: when they get hooked in to television to the exclusion of everything else, and become extremely hostile when you threaten to take it away. The answer, as all parents know really, is to set clear rules beforehand – to yourself as much as your children. Don't fall into the trap of allowing the TV to stay on longer than usual to buy more time for yourself – as soon as they sense this, it's much tougher to persuade them that they can't watch anymore.

Insist that their viewing time is allocated to certain hours of the day; never beyond lunchtime for example, or only after 5pm. Make it clear that they can never turn on the TV without asking you first and that it's not an automatic right as soon as they come home. If it's during the holidays, it is fine to allow them extra viewing hours as long as they don't exceed them, and structure in other activities too.

'Parents have to get the balance right, between one extreme where a child does nothing except watch TV, to the other, where it's too restrictive, so telly becomes a forbidden fruit and all the more attractive,' says says Dr Barrie Gunter, professor of mass communications at Leicester University. 'What you need to encourage is a mix of past times that they engage in during the day.'

What's so difficult is that the temptation is continual. Telly has progressed from the innocent world of the *Magic Roundabout*; thanks to digital TV, children's programmes are broadcast 24 hours a day, leaving it up to us to dictate what's off limits. It doesn't help that there always seems to be a new study linking children's viewing habits with raised cholesterol, obesity or aggressiveness and poor concentration. To ease our guilt, there is one strategy that psychologists view favourably, and that is sitting down with our children and watching it with them. 'Discussing what they're viewing plays a valuable role in children's learning,' says Dr Rachel Calam, a psychology lecturer at Manchester University who has researched children's television viewing habits. 'In fact, it's key. Content is less important because even if they are watching rubbish, you're there to explain to them how the advertiser is trying to sell them things. It helps them to become critical consumers.'

Gunter agrees, 'You've got to get children to think about television critically and positively. They need to know what they can enjoy about television, but also recognise that there are plenty of other ways of enjoying themselves too.' And they'll only do that by following your example. 'Parents do need to limit their viewing too,' advises Gunter. Only then will the kids be happy to forsake their square-shaped nanny and do something more interesting instead.

'Mummy, can I sleep in your bed?'
Joe, 4

It could be that Joe never sleeps in your bed and is merely inquisitive, in which case your answer could be as matter of fact as, 'There isn't enough room. We all have our own beds to sleep in, and Mummy and Daddy like their own space. You know you can come in with us if you're ill or for morning cuddles.' That should suffice.

If, however, Joe is a frequent visitor and you are attempting, probably not for the first time, to make a stand, then he is clearly going to raise an objection. To gain access to the parental bed is a position of power and privilege he won't relinquish easily, especially by the age of four years old. By the time they are able to creep into your bed unnoticed, it is much more difficult to stop them – physically at least. There are two reasons why most parents let it continue. At that time of night you're either too exhausted to put up a fight or you quite enjoy the closeness too; usually a mix of both.

'Often you find in this situation that one parent is saying to the other, "Don't you think this should stop?" and the other will say something like, "Come on. What's the harm? We shouldn't be so harsh,"' says Janet Reibstein, professor of psychology at Exeter University.

So where is the harm? If it brings comfort to all parties, why is it viewed so negatively by many childcare experts? It really comes down to boundaries. To what extent the child is allowed to get their own way and invade their parents personal space – and it doesn't get more personal than their bed – will affect other areas of discipline and autonomy too. 'Sharing a bed isn't just about being lovely, close and cuddly,' says Reibstein. 'It can be about tenderness and affection tipping over into dependence and reliance.' On both sides – not only the child's. 'You're not helping a child if you've become dependent on it. There are lines you may want to draw as a couple where you say, "This is our time for talking and being together."'

It can also be problematic if Joe can only associate falling asleep with being in his parents' bed – it takes away the opportunity for him to develop that crucial ability to fall asleep on his own. 'You need to ask, where does that child learn to be self-sustaining? Being able to fall asleep on your own is all about being able to soothe and calm yourself without the aid of others, which you need in all sorts of situations,' says Reibstein.

So, in answer to Joe, be firm, explain exactly why he can't but try to be sympathetic too. 'I would acknowledge how he feels,' says psychotherapist Sue Cowan-Jenssen. 'You can say, "Yes, it is nice, after all Mum and Dad sleep in the same bed. It is natural to want to but, No. You can't."' If the nocturnal visits still continue, a small reward to stay in his own bed each night for a week or two can often work wonders – although watch out that you don't start a whole new habit.

'Mummy, can I wear mascara to school?'
Abi, 10

Pre-teen requests can feel like a minefield because there are so few clear-cut rules. Who says young girls can't wear make-up and midriff-revealing clothes or emulate pop stars in MTV videos? Yet we feel uneasy that our ten year olds are marketed to in this way; encouraged to grow up so quickly. Candy-coloured lipgloss in pink packaging targeting children as young as four; slinky sequinned dresses for five year olds. Five years later, they're clamouring to buy mascara. So where – and when – do we draw the line?

According to a survey of nearly 6,000 girls from age seven to 19, carried out by consumer analysts Mintel, over 60% of primary school girls regularly wear make-up. At the school gates, primary schools take a strong line on make-up and jewellery and it's unlikely that they would permit Abi to wear any. It could be that one or two of her friends have managed to slip below the radar but you can simply defer to school policy on this – which makes it much easier for you to draw a clear line.

It is helpful to understand what mascara represents here – to you and to your daughter – in terms of growing up and experimenting. 'All make-up is shorthand for a growing sexuality,' explains Professor Lorraine Sherr, a clinical psychologist at University College London, specialising in women, gender and beauty. 'Mascara in particular is that innocent first step – the frontline, feminised product.' One that will undoubtedly open the floodgates to many more. No wonder it can make us feel uncomfortable. Us and the rest of society, says Sherr. 'Society does have a really clear rule about when it's too young – even if it isn't written down in black and white. Sometimes you only know a rule is a rule is when it is broken and wearing mascara to primary school is one of those.'

Even so, it is unfair to stop a ten year old wearing any make-up at all, particularly if she sees you applying it each day, or to go out in the evening. Rather than refusing her request, use it as a chance to share the experience, advises Dr Jennifer Leonard, psychologist and parenting coach. 'You could suggest going shopping and buying make-up together. You could talk to them about skincare and also budgeting – how much or little she could spend. Try to negotiate; say "no" to wearing it at school but be open to what they could wear at weekends – it's better to get her to co-operate than to do it behind your back.' Sherr agrees, 'At home you could let her try make-up out and frame it as, "Let's experiment together", so it's clearly earmarked.'

You could dabble with your own make-up together but try and keep it within the realms of play for as long as possible. You want them to feel that they haven't been denied a chance to explore their femininity, a learning curve that does, regardless of marketing, start at around ten years old. Sherr says, 'We want it to be a positive one, so see it as an opportunity to talk to a young girl around these issues – how she feels about her appearance and image, and about growing up to be a woman.'

'Mummy, can Eddie stay the night?'
Emily, 16

If you've never heard of Eddie, then this question will be one that requires good negotiation along with some expert detective skills. Of course you want to know, who on earth is he? What are his intentions? What are Emily's?

What such a question really doesn't require is a knee jerk reaction and a blanket refusal. If you can successfully navigate a question like this, there's much more chance she'll respect and confide in you in the future. The more honest and direct you can be from the outset, without causing her abject embarrassment, the better. 'The only way really is to be open about issues like contraception and sexually transmitted diseases; to seize the bull by the horns and discuss it,' says Kate Figes, author of *Terrible Teens – What Every Parent Needs To Know*. 'It all depends on how well you get on with your daughter and your own feelings towards sex,' she says.

The skill is digging around the question without appearing to be too intrusive. 'There have to be a few more questions when a teenager comes to you with this one,' says Gill Hines, education consultant and co-author of *Whatever!: A Down-to-Earth Guide to Parenting Teenagers*. 'Before you say yes or no, you want to know is it because Eddie can't get home? Where does she plan on him sleeping? How long have they known each other? You need to find out some intention in the nicest possible way. It's highly possible, they're just friends in which case, there's no reason to suppose that relationship will change.'

It would also help to know beforehand how you would feel if Emily did admit their sexual intentions. 'You're not going to be able to stop them having sex but if the thought makes you uncomfortable, you need to be honest about that,' says Hines. But if Emily says she wants him to sleep on the sofa, you have to take that as an honest statement and trust them.

Another dilemma is offering Eddie the spare room – is this a handy compromise or a way of avoiding talking about the issue altogether? 'I think parents who go for this are deluding themselves,' says Figes firmly. 'Everything goes on when you've gone to bed, so if you're going to allow them to stay the night, wherever it maybe, you need to face up to what that really means. Remember, there's no need for anyone to stay over. Unless they live 100 miles away, they can always get a cab home.'

The skill is being able to view our teenage children in a realistic way; not being naive about their sexual behaviour, or jumping to sensational conclusions either. As Figes says, 'Assume it's going to be more than they're letting on but it's never going to be as bad as you think it is.'

Realistically, whatever Eddie and Emily are up to – on the sofa or in the spare room – lies somewhere in between.

'Mummy, can I become a vegetarian?'
Rosie, 9

If you're a meat-loving parent, which presumably you are since your child needs to ask this question, the prospect of Rosie giving up meat isn't going to fill your heart with joy. How much easier to cook one meal for all the family without having to think of something clever to do with Quorn and lentils too. Then there's the added worry of nutrients and health. Still, you'd better get used to it – increasing numbers of children are becoming vegetarians because, like their parents, they're more aware of where their food, especially their meat, comes from and how it's been reared. Some children simply don't like the taste, others are more sensitive and become squeamish once they work out that Daddy's crispy bacon sandwich and the cute little piglet in *Babe* are one and the same.

Your first task is to find out why she's decided to raise the question – is it something they've seen on TV or been discussing at school? 'The chances are they are worried that eating meat is cruel and that's something you need to discuss with them,' says Calie Woozley, spokesperson for the RSPCA. 'If you're not keen on taking the vegetarian route, you could discuss the possibility of more free-range meat.'

Take her interest as an opportunity to talk about food production – where meat comes from, your own views on eating meat and how she feels about that. You could also discuss how it would fit in with your family lifestyle. 'Maybe you could try out one meat-free day a week to see how it goes and also to help the child feel that their parents are really listening,' says Woozley.

It will also help if you try not to view Rosie's possible conversion to vegetarian as an inconvenience; a rebellious stand against the family norm. If this is how you treat it, Rosie will only conform to your expectations and become more stubborn about it.

There is something indefinably reassuring about the ritual

of a communal family Sunday roast but there are alternatives. A vegetarian diet is one that can have a positive impact on the whole family's meals – and we already know it can be more healthy, even for younger children. Glenys Jones, nutritionist at MRC human nutrition research in Cambridge, says, 'There's no problem becoming a vegetarian even from five years old. It's fine to cut out meat as long as you replace it with other protein sources.' There are plenty you can substitute meat with, from tofu and Quorn to more eggs, milk, cheese, nuts, pulses and seeds. They also need plenty of fresh fruit and vegetables. If you do let Rosie alter her diet, then you also need to bear in mind that meals can take longer. 'Children have a high energy need and with foods like nuts, seeds and pulses, they need a bigger volume and it does take longer to digest them – maybe you should think about four smaller meals a day rather than three,' says Jones.

Finally, take comfort that Rosie's decision indicates that she is of superior intelligence – two years ago, the BMJ published research showing that children with higher IQs chose to become vegetarians. They were also more likely to be female, of a higher social class and better educated too.

What the study didn't indicate is whether they were motivated young cooks who liked to prepare their own meals – that would have been even more reassuring.

'Mummy, can I get my bellybutton pierced?'
Amy, 11

One minute they're begging for a *My Little Pony*, the next it's a diamond in their midriff. If one question crystalises your daughter's transition from child to tween, it is this. Sexuality, pure and simple, is at the root of such a dilemma. Whether your daughter is aware or not, there's no denying the purpose of this particular piercing – to draw one's gaze, inevitably male, to a certain area of the female body.

'It immediately makes you ask questions like how sexualised do you want your 11-year-old daughter to be?' says Kate Figes, author of *Terrible Teens*. However strongly you feel, it is worth trying to take her request seriously. Don't dismiss it out of hand. 'Deal with it as a real issue,' advises Claire Halsey, psychologist and parenting expert. 'Sit down with her and do it as a list of for's and against's. If, on balance, it's because she wants to be like her friends or part of the trend, ask "Is there any other way you can feel you're one of the group?" It's really about a calm and respectful approach.'

Remind her that members of the British Body Piercing Association won't carry out piercings on anyone under 14 years old and 14 to 16 year olds have to be accompanied by adults – so, officially, 11 is too young. 'Even so, it's important to talk it through because the danger is she may just go off and get it done herself,' says Suzie Hayman, a trustee for Parentline Plus. Also reassure yourself that there is no harm in just saying 'no', as Figes certainly would. 'Both mine were allowed to pierce their ears when they went to "big school" but I would say 11 is too young for belly button piercing.'

If you're taking a firm line, it can be helpful to play the health card – more credible than an emotional one. 'This is really about what age you feel they can have control over decisions about their own bodies. Depending on how you feel, you can say, "I am responsible for your health, education and safety and this is not something I consider safe for your welfare right now,"' says Figes. 'Your reaction in terms of whether it offends you isn't relevant. But you can argue that in terms of risk of infection and looking after the piercing, it's not suitable.'

Finally, encourage her to reflect on the implications and issues herself. Are you doing this because you want to look like your friends? Are you worried your friends would drop you if you didn't do this? Much better to help her to make these decisions in life rather than just say, 'No, you're a baby', says Hayman. Considering the options with her will mean that if and when you do say 'no', she's much more likely to respect you for it. You can also add that it would be much more painful than having her ears pierced; in this case, would she consider a clip-on belly ring instead?

'Mummy, why can't I smoke in my room?'
Sophie, 16

That Sophie is asking 'why not?' implies the boundary has already been set. So your first response could be 'why now?' Has she recently been to a more lenient household where the parents smoke too, or met a friend who is allowed these privileges? In contrast, of course, you will be held up as the most cruel and draconian parents imaginable.

Still, all you're trying to do is stick to your own house rules. 'They'll throw all sorts out there,' says Dr Rachel Andrew, a child psychologist who specialises in family issues. 'About their friends, and friends' Mums and Dads who say it's ok and how they're so much better, more lenient and liberal etc. But it's important to remember underneath they will be respecting and modelling the arguments you offer.' There are some pretty convincing health arguments when it comes to smoking, such as that cigarettes kill around 100,000 people before old age each year in Britain, from a wide range of deaths including heart attacks, strokes, gangrene, cancers of the mouth, throat, lung, kidney and bladder, and most of all from chronic obstructive lung disease.

If they don't appreciate the medical lecture you could say 'no', as Gill Hines, co-author of *Whatever!: A Down-to-Earth Guide to Parenting Teenagers*, advises because there is nowhere in the house where the smoke and smell wouldn't affect other family members.

Part of your reasoning depends upon how sacred you –or they – view their bedroom space. If it has always been viewed as their territory in which they can behave as they please, then it will be harder to set tough rules; an issue to start thinking about before you hit the potentially turbulent times of adolescence. 'I would view their room as still part of the house you inhabit. I don't feel the space is theirs – they have a lease on it. They'll move out one day and the bedroom will be yours again. So it's theirs – on certain conditions – as privilege and not a right,' says Hines.

Yet you can't be too intransigent – they are looking to you to learn the skills of compromise, listening and negotiation. 'Your child is testing out boundaries and listening to others' points of view,' says Andrew. 'Yes, it's good to show them that things can't always go their way but you also need to be flexible on some issues. That give and take is what keeps a loving relationship with your teenagers.' So if you really feel that banning Sophie from smoking in the house will only encourage her to smoke more somewhere else beyond your watchful eye, then negotiation is a better option. 'Is there another room in the house where you'd mind the smell less? You need to work out your bottom line and talk it through with your teenager from there,' says Andrew.

Hines agrees that a blanket 'no' isn't always ideal. 'There has to be an honest discussion and an acknowledgement, if it's the case, that someone is a smoker.' One reasonable compromise could be to smoke outside, a concept they'll be used to by now anyway. 'You could have a bench at the bottom of the garden,' says Hines. 'Hopefully it will deter them when the weather is cold and miserable but at least they won't be able to do it in the warmth and comfort of your own house.'

Some consolation, at least.

'Mummy, can I have a glass of wine too?'
Lauren, 14

With all the concern about teenagers and binge drinking, it is perplexing as a parent to know how permissive we can or should be. If Lauren gets a taste for spicy shiraz are we encouraging unhealthy drinking patterns later in life or, as many experts believe, introducing her to the concept of moderate drinking?

'My attitude would be to allow someone of Lauren's age a small taste of wine in a family context. I think responsible drinking around meal time is a different way of using alcohol; it's not necking it at happy hour with your peer group,' says psychologist Dave Spellman, specialising in teenagers and families. 'It is about helping them to bridge the gap between childhood and adulthood rather than making them wait until they're 18 years old when suddenly they can do what they want.'

This question should prompt us to reflect upon our own attitudes to alcohol and in what way we may be influencing our teenagers behaviour. According to a study out last year, 'Use of Alcohol Among Children and Young People', carried out by the Department for Children, Schools and Families (DCSF), one concern was how misinformed parents are about the dangers of alcohol, often because they enjoy drinking too.

A myth that persists is that the 'continental model' is best – we all idealise the drinking styles of countries like France and Italy, not least because it implies we can all continue bulk ordering from Majestic and not feel too guilty about it. What we don't hear so much about is the worrying levels of binge-drinking among young people over there too – so it doesn't appear to be a style that is working.

Another fallacy shared by parents is that getting drunk occasionally is part of a learning curve that allows us to drink more appropriately in the future. The principle being that downing a bottle of sweet sherry should put us off for life – it may have worked for us, but it doesn't seem to apply to this generation of teen drinkers. Otherwise they wouldn't keep doing it. 'One of the tragedies at the moment is the way we're treating drinking as a rite of passage, something we should expect from young teenagers,' says Professor Mark Bellis, director of public health at Liverpool John Moores University and a leading expert on young people and alcohol. 'There's a feeling that, "You're drinking again but there's not much I can do about that".'

One way forward, advises Bellis, predictable though it maybe, is to set really clear rules and stick to them. 'There's research coming out from the Netherlands that shows the importance of rules being enforced around alcohol – pinning down what you can and can't drink and not tolerating drunkeness,' says Bellis. Bear in mind that surveys also show at least 50% of the alcohol teenagers drink is supplied by parents. So it is fine to offer Lauren a glass of shiraz as long as it is accompanied with plenty of discussion and alcohol-related facts. 'They need to know not just about units but significant dangers around cancers, mental health, injuries and even educational performance,' says Bellis. 'Frank and informative communication is the only way.'

FAMILY MATTERS

'Mummy, will you marry me?'
Oliver, 5

When young Oliver looks into your eyes with idealistic adoration and pops the question, you can rest assured that your loving son is behaving exactly as he should for a five year old. Banish all anxieties of an indulged Mummy's boy, doomed to be living at home with you at the age of 41, à la Ronnie Corbett in *Sorry!*, if you encourage or entertain his romantic proposals.

'Around this time, many securely attached children ask this one and it's completely appropriate for their age,' says Dr Sharon Lewis, a psychologist specialising in parent-child attachment. 'It's a really good sign of a secure loving attachment – and it's also viewed as one of the best indicators of mental health later in life.'

The age of five is the peak for boys wanting to marry their mothers. 'It's that point just before they settle in at primary school and transfer the heat of their attention to their peer group; they're still at that stage when their parents – especially their mother – is their whole world,' says Lewis.

So it's a question that does need to be handled sensitively – endorsed rather than rebuked or ignored. 'You don't have to go into too much detail about why you can't marry him,' says

Lewis. 'Just be positive and say, "How lovely."'

Avi Shmueli, a therapist at the Anna Freud Centre of child and adolescent therapy, agrees. 'You can pick up on aspects of what was said rather than tackling the question straight on by saying, "Yes, that's fine – when you grow up you can marry me" or "That would be great but I am married to Daddy", and then worrying when he looks murderously rejected.'

It doesn't take a Freudian theorist to work out the Oedipal undertones but that doesn't mean such a question should be taken too literally. For starters, a five year old's concept of marriage bears no relation to our own. 'A child will use the word marriage to mean many different things,' he explains. 'It may be more realistic to think about it in terms of a child wanting to hold onto that parent and feel they can have them to themselves.' Or it could be more immediate than that. Maybe your child has spent an afternoon or day with you and he wants to prolong that attention. 'Think about the context in which it is said,' agrees Shmueli, who also believes that the Oedipal connection is still a relevant one. He says, 'It is a consideration here – Freud believed that it was very much related to a boy's sexual identity and developing a capacity to identify with their father as a male.' Part of which involves, inevitably, wishing they could marry like their Dad.

Relish this brief phase of uncritical adoration because it does pass quickly. A friend's six-year-old son used to propose to her at least once a week. That was a year ago. 'Now I remind him and he says, "Mum, I don't want to marry you anymore. Your hands are too wrinkly. I think I'll marry someone younger instead."'

'Mummy, why does Granny look like she needs ironing?'
Anya, 7

Or to translate Anya's childlike perspicacity, why is Granny so wrinkly? Questions like this can make us feel uncomfortable; is pointing out granny's sagging skin innocent curiosity or is something more negative lurking? Are they absorbing and reflecting back, perhaps, our own hidden distaste and fears?

Firstly, dealing with the question itself is easier if you have the simple facts to hand. 'Granny has more wrinkles than we do because of cell loss. You could say that our cells, which make us what we are, reproduce themselves a certain amount of times and then they die,' explains Professor Ian Stuart-Hamilton, who specialises in the psychology of ageing. 'So the less elastic and the more thin the skin becomes.' You could then do the skin age test with them as a way of illustrating how cells diminish. 'Pinch a pyramid on the back of your hand and let go. When Granny does it, you could go away and make a cup of tea and it will still be working it's way back,' predicts Stuart-Hamilton. When your child does it, it will spring down enviably quickly. This rapidly leads us on to how we feel about ageing. How can we be that positive, or expect our children to be too, about dying cells and baggy skin that refuses to snap back to where it should be? 'I think you can be positive and, anyway, you should tell the truth – you may as well know what you're up against,' says Stuart-Hamilton, who also believes it is crucial to challenge any early signs of ageism. 'It's one of the dumbest prejudices anyone can have since you'll inevitably end up being the thing you despise, and the evidence shows that those who have strong stereotypes about old age are the most miserable when they are old.'

You could start by discussing their own physical changes as a comparison. 'Explain that everyone changes as they get older,' says Dr Jane Prince, a psychologist specialising in changes in identity across the life span. 'You could say, "Well, look at the way you've developed in the last seven years, how you've grown hair and your face is a different shape". You could look at their baby pictures and photos of when their Mum and Dad were younger to show that we're all going through a similar process.' If you feel your child is anxious about the thought of ageing, you can reassure them – and yourself – that contrary to all those gloomy dementia statistics you read, there is no real evidence, according to Stuart-Hamilton, that old age is all that bad for you. 'There was a lovely study done in the '80s comparing young and old chess players,' says Stuart-Hamilton. 'The young were quicker but, when young and old were matched on handicap, the older players drew on that extra experience to compensate for loss of raw processing power.'

So, you can tell Anya, you may lose a bit of wit but you gain a lot of wisdom. Or you could always quote the late humorist and author Miles Kington. 'Intelligence is knowing that a tomato is a fruit. Wisdom is knowing not to put it in a fruit salad.'

'Mummy, do you love my sister more than me?' Kitty, 6

We yearn for sibling harmony and not just because it makes our jobs as parents so much easier. In those rare minutes when our young children display mutual love and protectiveness, it feels like we've done our job well, that we've been able to achieve the impossible in giving them the attention they crave.

As Vicki Iovine, bestselling parenting author of the *Girlfriends' Guide To...* says, 'Just when you think you can't take another step, out of the corner of your eye you will see the toddler child hug his new baby brother or sister like he really means it, and you will weep and hear angels sing.'

In contrast, we begin to question our parenting skills when we're umpiring jealous spats and stemming the flow of their constant accusations, in particular; 'You love her more than you love me, don't you?' 'Inevitably they will say this and parents tend to respond very deeply,' says Dr Terri Apter, child psychologist and author of *The Sister Knot: Why We Fight, Why We're Jealous and Why We'll Love Each Other No Matter What.* 'They feel the moral quality of their parenting is on the line.' What one should remember is that the battle for parental love isn't necessarily a bad thing. 'They will always measure themselves against one another but this isn't destructive or a sign that they'll be unhappy,' says Apter. 'Instead it helps to tell them who they are, encouraging siblings to define themselves in different ways.'

Although when a child does ask such a question, it is really an invitation for reassurance. 'Accept the invitation. They need answers,' says Jan Parker, family psychotherapist and co-author of *Raising Happy Brothers and Sisters.* 'Most children can understand short-term differences in parental attention if the reasons are explained ("He can't do things for himself like you can", "She's having a tough time at school so I'll need some time alone with her to chat things through") and they feel noticed, appreciated and loved themselves.'

Also don't shy away from talking about the nature of love.

As Parker says, 'Many children fear that love is like a cake – if someone else has a slice there's less for them. Explaining parental love – that it is something precious and unique that grows between a parent and each child, that it is theirs and something others can't take away – can ease very real worries.'

In terms of reassuring yourself, view it as healthy and positive that your child feels able to ask such a question. 'It's a sign that she feels she can be honest,' says psychologist Linda Blair, who specialises in sibling relationships. 'It's good that she is able to express herself, which means she must feel safe with her mother.' Finally, don't feel guilty that you only have finite energy for each of your children. 'It's not a sign that you don't love your daughter enough,' says Apter. 'Remember that she's learning a very important lesson about learning to share and compete in a world with other people.'

'Mummy, everyone else has got a brother or sister, why haven't I?'
Liam, 7

Liam could be asking this question purely in the spirit of curiosity, as in, why is the sky blue? In which case, his query demands a fairly honest answer.

'I would give a reply as close as the truth that you can,' advises Dr Richard Woolfson, child psychologist and author of *Why do kids do that?* 'You could say, for example, "We love you so much we want to give you all of our attention right now", or "We'd like you to have another brother or sister but it's difficult for us for physical reasons". And you need to find a way of communicating that to your child.'

Alternatively, Liam could be asking this question – and the phrasing implies as much – if he feels a little hard done by. At seven years old, he could be comparing himself to other friends with siblings, and feeling unusual. Your task is to promote the positive aspects of being an only child. If you do feel guilty or upset about not being able to have more children, it's crucial to be encouraging. 'It's so important to make him feel he's not missing out,' says Woolfson. 'Even if you're yearning for another one, you need to stress the good aspects, the advantages of his position. You could say something like, "You may think it's great they've got brothers and sisters but they do fight and take each other's toys – aren't you lucky you haven't got that?"'

What you also want to avoid is over-empathising with your child, says Woolfson, as in, 'I know, if only you could have a sibling – I feel exactly the same way,' suggesting that a one-child family is a rather miserable alternative. There's certainly no evidence that this is the case, which could also be a comfort to Liam. In the UK, the percentage of women having one child has more than doubled in the last ten years from ten to 23 per cent, so it is clearly becoming more of a norm than a lonely alternative. There are other advantages too that you could explain to Liam; one significant analysis of existing research, carried out in the mid-1980s, showed that only-children were, if anything, better off in terms of academic achievement, motivation and self-esteem.

Even so, it is also important to strike a balance here; acknowledging your only child's sense of difference, not just dismissing it with positive spin. If it's the underlying root of Liam's question, it needs to be explored. 'My main perspective is that it *is* different being an only child,' says Bernice Sorensen, therapist and author of *Only-child experience and adulthood.* 'They can feel they're missing out and how you deal with that is very important. I'm an only child too and I do think we see the world in a different way,' says Sorensen. 'There can be a sense of aloneness but it doesn't necessarily mean loneliness.'

It could simply be that Liam craves more company. 'Ask yourself, do they have enough playtime with other children in place?' advises Sorensen. If that's the solution, it's rather easier to arrange than an extra sibling.

'Mummy, if I didn't come from your tummy, where did I come from?
Lucy, 4

It's never too early to start talking to an adopted child about where they came from. These days most adopted children will have a 'Life Story Book', containing details of where they were born, their background and their birth parents. But they will still rely on you for most of the answers, especially if they were adopted at a very young age.

'Start as young as possible,' advises Patricia McGinty, child placement consultant for the British Association for Adoption & Fostering (BAAF). 'Pre-school is the ideal age. We know from research that children introduced to the concept of adoption as young as toddlers, learn to accept the term as fact much more easily, like their hair colour and their gender.' Telling an adopted child early on is also important in case they hear it from someone else; a sibling or another family member. Susan Dronyk, a psychotherapist specialising in adoption issues, agrees. 'Once you have introduced it, don't shut the subject away again. You also need to be clear and open without telling them anything too disturbing. It is a balancing act but try to remember the alternative. I've seen so many people over the years who weren't told honestly about their background and it can be devastating to find out later on; it's a huge shock to them if they feel a secret has been kept from them.'

Even if they lack an in-depth understanding at such a young age, it doesn't matter. Developmentally they are already learning to attach positive and negative values to issues – including their own adoption. So when Lucy asks about her origins, you should be encouraging and straightforward. McGinty suggests: 'I would say, "You came out of another lady's tummy. Her name was – and give her name if you know it – and she was unable to look after you." You could add, "She tried very hard to look after you and loved you very much. We wanted a child of our own and so you came to live with us. We were so happy, we had a special party."' Crucially, you can say that just because she's adopted doesn't mean she is any less loved than a child who is with her birth parents. At this point, don't feel you have to offer too many facts. What's more important is conveying a sense that you feel relaxed talking to her, that adoption isn't an awkward or taboo issue. 'It's important right from the start to be aware of your own feelings,' says McGinty. 'If you're not at ease with your child's background or with your role as an adoptive parent, they will pick up on that,' she says. A parent who feels comfortable and accepting about their child's adoption will help their child to feel the same way too.

'Mummy, is it ok to love Daddy more than you?'
Martha, 5

Not only is it ok for Martha to adore her Daddy, it is a crucial phase in her emotional development. Nonetheless, it can be a little bruising for a mother's ego when Daddy is so high up on the pedestal that nothing can knock him from first place. Or as Elizabeth Hartley-Brewer, child development specialist and author of *Raising and Praising Girls* puts it, 'Fathers become Gods to their daughters in a way that mothers never become Goddesses.' However much you feel you deserve to be, if it's anything like my household you're more likely to be told, 'Mummy, you stink. Where's my Daddy?'

So the correct demeanour when Martha drives home, yet again, how low your popularity has sunk is cool, neutral and supportive, accompanied by the words, 'That's absolutely fine, darling. It's important to love more than one person. We will always love you however you feel about each of us.'

Reassure yourself this isn't personal, Hartley-Brewer agrees: 'It's not a rejection of you as an individual but a natural stage all girls pass through. It is necessary for the child to develop that intimate attachment to the other parent; it's part of moving across, so they are freed up from their reliance on mother as a key carer.'

It is also important to understand the question from a child's perspective, rather than your own. Recognise that five-year-old Martha isn't using the word 'love' in the same way that you would. 'Don't attach too much meaning to it,' says Hartley-Brewer. 'Children are very immediate and they are expressing the feeling that is most powerful to them at that moment. Not necessarily one that is permanent. Maybe they've had a nice day or a nice week with Daddy and it's the feeling they're filled with at that time,' she says.

Remind yourself that it is perfectly normal for a child at this age to display favouritism. But why? Dr Avi Shmueli, a therapist at the Anna Freud Centre for child and adolescent therapy, explains, 'At this stage a child is exploring where she stands in terms of her parents. It is the theme of exclusion and inclusion that Freud referred to in his theory of the Oedipus Complex. It's all about the triad – the triangle between the parents and child – and the child's struggle to deal with feelings of being left out that extend right into adulthood.'

It is the same for boys and girls, although girls will experience it differently. 'There is a key difference,' says Hartley-Brewer. 'Girls can go on loving their fathers forever, feeling a real passion for them and that's normal. Yet boys will move away from their mothers, usually around the age of eight years old.' The allure of Dads, she says, is their perceived power. 'It comes down to the father figure as ultimate protector,' she says.

Still there are advantages. Loving Daddy so devotedly means that he is now first choice when she stamps her foot and demands that someone dress her or take her to the loo in a crowded restaurant, and wipe her bottom if he's lucky. Such is the price of adoration.

'Mummy, if we're identical, how can we be different?' Lily and Louisa, 8

The critical issue for every identical twin is how they can achieve individuality. If they look in the mirror and see their identical sister's reflection staring back at them, separation must, at times, feel like a challenge. Yet identical twins who are raised together, you can explain to Lily and Louisa, are far more likely to be different from one another than those who are separated at birth. 'The ones who grow up together make a conscious effort, especially around the age of seven or eight years old, to establish their own identity. Studies show that, in contrast, twins who've never known one another tend to choose similar partners and go into similar professions,' says Emma Mahony, mother of twins and author of *Double Trouble: Twins and How To Survive Them*.

You can also reassure yourself that however much our DNA may define physical appearance, it can only go so far with personality. 'Even though identical twins will have the same genes, the way their genes function – their expression – will be influenced by environmental factors and random events,' says Professor Michael Rutter, professor of developmental psychopathology at the Institute of Psychiatry. 'Importantly, genes aren't everything – there will be developmental factors. Every twin is still a unique individual.'

Yet it can be tricky for parents knowing how best to encourage that uniqueness. According to Audrey Sandbank, honorary consultant for TAMBA (Twins and Multiple Births Association) and psychotherapist, a habit parents can fall into is saying one twin is good at 'x' and the other is good at 'y'. She says, 'You often find that twins divide their personalities between them; if one is good at reading or making decisions, the other will drop that skill, and the parent makes it worse by encouraging this.' Parents assume this type of pigeonholing is helping twins to separate; in fact, it can create even more co-reliance. Identical twins can end up 'sharing' a set of personality traits rather than developing as a whole person and relating to the world as an individual.

However, this isn't inevitable and there are ways parents can avoid it, says Sandbank. 'Although it can be tempting for a busy parent, it's important not to let twins look after one another. One can end up caring for another, or they can both team up and it is easy for parents to back down in the face of twin power. It's important to take control early on,' she says.

Parents need to be able to interact with each of their twins as individuals and spending quality one-to-one time with them is a crucial aspect. Sandbank recommends starting them at pre-school on alternate days, so one stays at home with their parent while the other learns to relate to their teacher on their own. 'In this way they can learn to see themselves as "I" instead of "We",' she says.

'Mummy, can I kiss my cousin?'
Iris, 6

It is perfectly normal for Iris to be drawn to her first cousin, especially at a young age. If both families see each other regularly, she may well view him affectionately like a brother, except one with the added sense of otherness and novelty rolled in.

She may even ask if she can marry him; another way of expressing how fond she is of him, how much she enjoys being with him. You could start by saying, 'Of course you can kiss your cousin' and affirm her affectionate feelings. 'It's so nice that you like him – he's such a lovely boy' and keep it simple. She may wonder if other people ever marry their cousins and the simple answer is, yes – a lot more than we ever really realise. Indeed Britain has a tradition of 'kissing cousins' going back hundreds of years.

Charles Darwin famously married his cousin Emma and went on to have ten children. Other first cousin couples include H.G. Wells and Isabel Mary, and Queen Victoria and Prince Albert, along with many of the royal family at that time. It is only in more recent times that the bond makes us feel uncomfortable. When the actor Greta Scacchi fell in love with her first cousin, Carlo, and had a son in 1998, it was frowned upon by everyone from the tabloids to the Catholic church.

Traditionally cousins married to keep wealth in the family – although poor families were keen too. 'You used to get more in the higher echelons of society,' explains Professor Alan Bittles, a geneticist at Murdoch University, Perth, Australia. 'Big wealthy families would have kept things together through cousin marriages. In this way you would have felt more secure – keeping family secrets, as well as money, close to you.'

At the other extreme, it was a way of *saving* money. 'You would get families who were unable to afford a dowry, which they wouldn't then have to pay if their daughter married a cousin, and it was a benefit if the girl knew her mother-in-law. So there were reckoned to be considerable social and economic advantages,' says Bittles.

It is still perfectly legal here but the general feeling is it's a bit close to home, unhealthy, incestuous even. Genetically the health risks are low. The chance of a child inheriting genetic disorders rises from around two per cent in the general population to four per cent if the parents are cousins. In other words, cousins have a 96% chance of producing a normal baby. Yet a taboo remains. 'Psychologically there is a sense of revulsion which springs from what society decides is taboo; in this case, cousins being too much like brother or sister,' says Janet Reibstein, professor of psychology at Exeter University, 'As families have spread out, I think overtones of any type of sibling intimacy, which cousins hint at, becomes more disturbing.'

What attracts Iris – that feeling of familiarity and being closely related, maybe even looking like each other – makes us feel uneasier as adults. Not that you should convey any of these doubts to Iris – it is lovely to feel close to a cousin and would be a shame to discourage her feelings in any way. No doubt she will eventually grow out of her affections but until then let her emulate Queen Victoria and Darwin, and be a kissing cousin.

THE DEEP STUFF

'Mummy, if there's a God, why are there so many wars?'
Patrick, 9

After marvelling at your child's sparkling intellectual curiosity, you may well feel slightly daunted by a question that, after several centuries, still baffles theologians and philosophers. Don't feel inadequate that you cannot reach for concrete answers. It is useful for Patrick to learn about the nature of uncertainty and that many questions are open-ended, often raising yet more imponderables.

Philosopher and author Julian Baggini advises, 'I would begin by asking the child what they think; using it as a way of starting a discussion. If parents can't give clear-cut answers, they feel they're failing their kids but it's a great mistake to assume children can't cope with uncertainties; it's important that they learn that there aren't straightforward answers to everything and not feel paralysed by that.'

You could ask Patrick if there's a particular reason he's asked this now? Does he believe in God? If so, can he think of any reasons that he may allow war? What you feel yourself, and the direction you may steer Patrick towards, will depend upon your own spiritual beliefs. If you're an non-believer, like A.C. Grayling, author and professor of philosophy at the

University of London, you'll have no problem pointing out, as he did to his own children, 'There are no Gods, only people; people are a mix of good and bad, though most people are mostly good. Wars come from the bad things that people think and do, which makes the governments of their countries quarrel with one another – and sometimes those sorts of grown-up quarrels use guns and bombs, and that is very destructive and bad.'

If, however, you have a faith and hope your child will too, you will probably want to offer a persuasive justification as to why God has remained resolutely silent throughout the thousands of wars that have shaped mankind. Catholic broadcaster and author Peter Stanford patiently explains to his children that, 'Good religion is what stops us having wars. The golden rule is never do unto others what you wouldn't want done unto yourself. If we followed that rule, there would be no wars based on religion. I would also say that if you're looking for one thing throughout history that has encouraged us to put people first, and not ourselves, it's religion.' Although, if Patrick is particularly savvy, he could point out that religion can't be that effective at stopping wars since there are still 30 major wars being fought around the globe at the moment.

You could point out that God gave people free will – going to war is our choice and we have to take responsibility and learn from the consquences. Patrick may well ask why God didn't create nicer people in the first place, that weren't hardwired to be territorial. To which you could respond, if everyone was only capable of being nice or good, they wouldn't be so free – they would be rather one-dimensional beings instead.

Philosophical counsellor Tim LeBon, suggests, 'If that doesn't satisfy him you could always quote Woody Allen who says, "If it turns out there is a God, I don't think he's evil. The worst you can say about him is that basically he's an underachiever."'

See what Patrick thinks of that.

'Mummy, what is a soul?'
Daniel, 8

Thankfully this is a question that really doesn't require a single answer – how could it? So don't even attempt to give one. 'I would resist defining what it is,' says Karen Aylward, a lecturer on children's thinking in religious education at Exeter University. 'Instead I would very much explore what *they* think it is and use their ideas as a starting point. I'd want to know why they've asked the question; is it something they've seen on television, linked to a question at school, or are they curious about what happens to us after we die?'

Once you've established the context, you will probably find yourself trying to describe that indefinable essence of someone that we can't actually see. You could start by saying that the soul is the immaterial or unphysical part of ourselves – our thoughts, feelings, imagination and personality. 'The obvious answer, you could say, is it's the bit that makes us who we are,' says philosopher and author Julian Baggini. 'Aristotle believed that the soul is a form of a living thing – it's about being alive in the fullest way possible and that if you don't really function properly, if you're living badly or being evil, then you don't really have a soul.' In this sense, soul can also have a moral implication – to be 'soulless' is to be lacking in heart, substance, principle or meaning.

You could add that people from religious and spiritual backgrounds feel that the soul is a part of us that lives on after death. 'Some people talk about their soul as the breath of God within them,' says Aylward. 'Others feel it's the bit that connects us to something bigger; it's a universal thing we all share. The key to emphasise is that there are many different ways of understanding what a soul could be.' And that just because we can't touch it or see it, doesn't mean it's not there. 'A child may ask, "Well, if you can't see it, then how do you know it's there?"' says Aylward. 'You could say, "There are other things we know about but can't see, like the wind – but we can see its effects. Or feelings – we know they're there, even if we can't see them."'

You could try talking about how the soul is represented in different areas of popular culture. 'Start with where they're at,' agrees Aylward. 'For instance, there's one episode of *The Simpsons* where Bart sells his soul. You could use that as a discussion point of how the soul helps us to think about right and wrong. The Tormentors in Harry Potter suck the soul, or the living essence, out of people which is another way in to it.'

Or you could talk about the soul in other contexts – why we often refer to art forms, certain types of music as having 'soul' and why this could be.

'Then again, you could also follow that principle in philosophy where you show by example,' says Baggini. 'In which case, I'd just be tempted to put on a James Brown album and say, "That's soul."'

'Mummy, why can't I live forever?'
George, 8

You could start with some gentle comparisons to ease yourself into this scientific minefield – otherwise known as the evolution of ageing. Begin in a general way with other examples in nature, as in, 'Well, George, everything lives for a certain amount of time, peaks and then fades. It's a pattern you see everywhere from plants to animals – even your pet goldfish – and it includes humans. Humans are only really designed to live long enough to look after their children and then make way for the next generation.' If there's an insistent 'But why?' then it's time for a simple biology lesson. 'Our body is made up of cells and when they reach a certain age and can't duplicate themselves perfectly, they die off,' explains Professor Ian Stuart-Hamilton, who specialises in the psychology of ageing. 'If cells were immortal and could still duplicate even when they're damaged, it would be like photocopying a bad print over and over again.'

In this scenario, all sorts of nasty diseases from muscle weakening to cancer would thrive more successfully than they do already. 'It's too hideous a thought to contemplate,' says Stewart-Hamilton. But what if George sensibly inquires why those cells have to decline and grow damaged in the first place? The simple answer is that no-one can really agree why all living things must weaken and die. Some argue that because nature is a highly competitive place and most animals die before old age – which explains why you never see geriatric animals running about in the wild – there simply hasn't been a biological need to keep the body healthy forever. Until now, which is why other scientists, as we speak, are busily extending the lifespan of yeast fungus by altering their genetic make-up, and believe that an 800-year lifespan is just one genome away. You could also point out that if you look at Japan, we're halfway to immortality already. 'In the last 40 years, the life expectancy there for women has gone up and up,' says Professor Felicia Huppert, director of the Wellbeing Institute at Cambridge University. 'At every stage, scientists have argued it would level off but there's no sign of that yet – already the average age expectancy is 85.' And that's increasing by three months each year.

You could, finally, ask George why immortality is such a great idea anyway. Presumably it would only really appeal to him if all his friends and loved ones could live forever too – and then the world would be a very crowded place. 'It is an idea that raises yet more questions,' says Huppert. 'You could suggest that although it's wonderful doing things for the first time, after you've done them several thousand times wouldn't it become less interesting?' Stewart-Hamilton agrees. 'If we knew we had forever, we'd lose that sense of urgency; that great spark that drives us,' he says. 'Look at the Galapagos tortoises. They famously have an average life expectancy of over 200 years. But they don't half lead boring lives – what, really, is the point?'

'Does God have a Mummy?'
Evie, 6

Typically this is a rather female question – at six years old, Evie will be much more curious than, say, her younger brother in exactly how we our related to one another and whose tummy we sprang from. So she may well start wondering at around this age who is Mummy to the biggest Daddy of them all. Not that there are any logical answers. If you hope that Evie will grow up believing in God, then you've got some explaining to do. Even leading theologists struggle to know what to tell a six year old. 'Well, in a straightforward way you could say God is seen as the source of absolutely everything. God doesn't need a Mummy or Daddy because he isn't human – he doesn't get older and he's never been a child. But he is like a father to us and a parent. There's not a lot more you can say to clarify it,' says Dr Mike Higton, a senior lecturer in theology at the University of Exeter.

Pretty much all the major religions agree that there was nothing before God and that he exists outside the limits of time. Higton agrees: 'There is no one point when God came into being – this is a much harder idea to explain to a child although it's pretty fundamental to religious thinking.'

You could try to appeal to a child's innate sense of logic and explain the case philosophically. As philosophical counsellor Tim LeBon says, 'God couldn't have a mother because he's the Creator. But if for some reason he did, then his mother would be God and if she had a mother, that being would be God. To avoid an infinite regress, we have to have a being or entity that doesn't have a mother.'

Another approach is to ask Evie how she visualises God – seeing him in a different way could help her to grapple with the complex nature of God's parentage – or lack of it. LeBon says, 'Any child who asks this probably views God as a kindly figure living in the clouds, a sort of celestial Dumbledore. To understand this question, you could ask them to look at Him in another way ie. God as everywhere and everything.'

If Evie looks confused, and who wouldn't, it is probably

better to digress and mention that she isn't the first one to suggest that God could have a Mummy. Some theologians have argued that Mary is God's mother. In the early history of the Church, she was even referred to by some as the Mother of God. Higton explains, 'In Christianity, Jesus is seen as God's human form – showing us what God is like. So there is a sense, you could say, in which God does have a mother.'

There is the atheist option but don't view this as an easy way out of a tough question. If you tell Evie that God is only a story, that leaves the Big Bang. Before you know it, you're back to the same old conundrum; what came before that? As LeBon says, 'God doesn't solve the problem but take him away and you still don't have the answers.'

'Mummy, can I fly to heaven?'
Meera, 6

Whether you are religious or not, Meera's query touches on profound questions we formulate even at a very young age about heaven and its precise location; can you reach it by easyJet or by being good, and why is it always presumed to be somewhere 'up there'? Geographically it makes sense to have something above us to which we can aspire; an elevated state of being.

But it is really the Church that has encouraged the traditional notion of viewing heaven in such a concrete, rather than abstract, way; all those images of God in his flowing white robes comes from the pulpit and earliest Western Christian art. 'It was to give Medieval people a sense of the tangible,' agrees Catholic broadcaster and author Peter Stanford. 'It's only when they invented telescopes and astronomy, that people could see heaven wasn't out there.' Still, argues Stanford, it is these images and poetic language that expresses our longing for, somewhere up there, something that transcends the concrete. 'And really it has got to be beyond our imagination hasn't it?', he argues. 'If it wasn't, it wouldn't be worth it. It would be, as Mark Twain once said, "A cheap little ten-cent heaven."'

Even as an atheist or agnostic, it seems churlish to dissuade a young child that heaven, either as a place or a concept, exists.

Whatever your beliefs, it's a nice way of encouraging your child's imagination and their ability to grapple with the abstract. 'Children need to use the language of the imagination,' says Dr Douglas Hedley, a lecturer in the philosophy of religion at Cambridge University. 'On the one hand it's crass to think of transcendence as "up there" and yet it's good to hold onto those childlike notions. With maturity and reflection you don't think of it as crudely as that. The mind is complicated and it's healthy to be able to integrate these different layers of meaning.'

One should point out that you can't literally fly there, says Dr Morwenna Ludlow, a lecturer in theology, at Exeter University. 'I think I'd be inclined to be honest – it's fine to say, "You can't get there now and there's a lot we don't know about heaven". In fact it's reassuring to know that it's ok not to know everything – much better than giving them platitudes about poor old granny up there in heaven.'

Explaining heaven to a child via their imagination is often the easiest way, the only way in fact. 'You could talk about books and computer games,' suggests Ludlow. Get them thinking about worlds that feel very real to them – Harry Potter could be a good example – that are logically organised but you can't actually get to from here. Then I'd suggest heaven was similar – a shared place we all understand in our mind.'

But not really somewhere you can use a map or a ladder to reach.

'Mummy, is it wrong to kill ants?'
Kai, 7

Fine if Kai has accidentally trodden on an ant walking up the garden path but rather different if he's jumping on them, gleefully committing mass genocide with the stamp of a foot, and relishing the power. If this is the case, you should swiftly stop Kai from his mindless killing spree and try, if you can, to appeal to his empathetic side.

Bearing in mind that quote from *King Lear*, 'As flies to wanton boys are we to th' gods; they kill us for their sport', you could say, how would he feel if an enormous foot the size of a stadium appeared towering over his head, and wiped out his friends, family and community in a few seconds – for no reason other than pleasure? How would that make him feel? He will probably find the comparison amusing but it is a good way of introducing a sense of scale and perspective.

Despite their size, you can explain, these tiny creatures are to be admired. They have colonised almost every landmass on earth and have developed impressively sophisticated societies where, you could say, their colonies are like vast families – in which everyone works together for the good of the whole rather than themselves.

Kai could say, 'What if the "good of the whole" means invading our kitchen and eating our food?', in which case, he's got a point. You would have to be honest and say, in that circumstance, it is acceptable to kill them to protect our food and keep the kitchen clean and hygienic.

You can argue that what makes it right or wrong – good or bad – is one's personal intention. Did Kai want to kill those ants to protect the kitchen or just because he could? This is where one would have to draw a moral line.

'The key word here is harmlessness,' says Bryan Appleyard, vice-president of the British Buddhist Society. 'As much as possible try to avoid causing harm but also realise that in practical terms you can't avoid killing living things. Even if you take an antibiotic, you're ending life by killing off bacteria. But I would say you can know that and still respect all living things.'

It is the spirit in which you act that counts, emphasises Appleyard. 'If there's a plague of ants in your house, you'll use ant powder, naturally. As long as it's not gratuitous.' Jack Cohen, reproductive biologist and honorary mathematics professor at the University of Warwick, agrees, 'Every time we swallow we kill lives – small amoeba that live in our mouth and throat. But that doesn't mean we should kill anyway. The fact that there are car accidents doesn't allow us to murder.'

You may exert more influence over Kai by simply impressing upon him that ants are pretty cool as insects go. Look how often they turn up in fables and children's stories to represent social cohesion, co-operation and industriousness – most recently and successfully *Antz* and *A Bug's Life*. If all else fails, you could always paraphrase Samuel Johnson: 'Turn on the prudent ant thy heedful eyes. Observe her labours, sluggard, and be wise.'

'Mummy, who would care for me if you died?' Sarah, 5

Young children will ask variations of this question for all sorts of different reasons. It isn't a sign of insecurity or an overly

114

anxious temperament but more a natural curiosity and developing awareness that none of us will be around indefinitely. There's no way of protecting them from this harsh reality nor any reason why you should wish to.

Even though they may not fully understand the true concept of death, by five years old they are beginning to grasp the idea that, generally, younger people live longer than older people. Around the same time they may show a marked interest in your age compared to their own, counting out their diminutive years on one hand and marvelling at how quickly they run out of fingers when you tell them that you are 40.

Swiftly enough they put two and two together and realise that you will die before them. Firstly reassure Sarah that it's highly unlikely such an event will happen while they are young but acknowledge how awful it would feel for them if it did. 'The terror here is abandonment,' says psychotherapist Sue Cowan-Jenssen. 'It's helpful to talk about all the other people around her who love her – granny, grandpa, aunty, godmother etc – so they feel they wouldn't be left alone if the worst were to happen.'

You could say simply that Mummy doesn't intend to die for a long time and try to leave it at that. 'Don't give them too lengthy an explanation,' agrees Dr Carol Burniston, consultant child psychologist specialising in bereavement and loss. 'You can make it all too complicated which shows too much anxiety about the issue on the part of the parent.'

What they find difficult to grasp is that when the dreaded time arrives, they will no longer depend on you, let's hope, as they do now. Cowan-Jenssen says, 'They think they'll feel the same way when they're grown up. We know that you don't feel helpless and alone in the world if you're an adult when your parents die. This can be stated quite concretely,' she says. 'You could say, "Right now you need Mum and Dad but that will change."' It is difficult for them, developmentally, to make this abstract leap and imagine what it could feel like, so you could talk about your own experiences. Whether or not your own parents have died, you could say, 'I've got my own family now and that makes me feel safe, loved and secure – just as you will have when Daddy or I finally die.'

Most children, says Burniston, will be happy with a simple reassurance and then you can divert them, ideally, with a discussion on how to keep ourselves healthy. Which at least offers them – and you – a semblance of control. 'You can turn it around into something that's quite positive,' says Burniston. 'Talk about your own wellbeing: "We eat healthy food, we exercise etc – this is what we do to look after ourselves and make sure we all live well – and for as long as possible."

'Mummy, is it ok to lie?'
Alex, 7

You could say 'No' but we all know that this would be a white lie in itself – and Alex, like most children, would see through it pretty quickly. She could say, 'What about last week when you told Granny you loved the book she bought you and you didn't tell her you had it already?' By seven years old, children have grasped the complexity of lying. They can distinguish between white lies – the sort we tell Granny to protect her feelings – and unacceptable dishonesty. It is important to be honest about degrees of lying and to be aware that deception is something that we all learn at an early age to facilitate social harmony. 'We all do it and if you give blanket rules not to lie, it may not work,' says leadership psychologist Averil Leimon. 'Very rigid rules limit the child's ability to reason it out for themselves. Like everyone, they will be learning the subtle skills of white lies because they don't want to hurt other people's feelings.'

Why, one wonders, is Alex asking this? Does she suspect someone has told her a lie? Or is she upset she may have told a 'bad' lie rather than a white lie? You could start to discuss the different types of lies and encourage her to give examples. Ask them what they think about lying – when have they ever wanted to tell lies and why. 'Because there is some incongruity and there are grey areas here, it is a conversation that you need to keep having,' says Leimon.

Dr Helen Rodwell, a child psychologist specialising in family and children, says, 'You can say that, by and large, we don't lie to people but white lies can be acceptable. You can talk about those situations when we don't want to upset people – if a friend asks if her hair looks nice and you think it looks awful, there's good reason not to tell her what you really think.' You could say there are lies to avoid punishment or being 'found out' and lies told with the genuine desire to protect another's feelings.

It is worth knowing that the latter type of lie is a key milestone in a child's development and an indication of emotional intelligence. Psychologists often refer to the Theory of Mind, when children move away from an egocentric state – around four years old – and start to understand that others have desires, intentions and beliefs that are different to their own, ie. Granny loves her blue-rinse poodle perm even though you don't.

From about six years old, they understand the social consequences of lying and are perfectly able to distinguish between truth and fiction. Sometimes referred to as Machiavellian intelligence, this is also the age when they can, if they wish to, lie extremely convincingly. Which goes hand in hand with a growing awareness of that dividing line between what they think privately and what they choose to express publicly –a life skill that Alex will be starting to hone right now. Let's hope not too successfully. Bear in mind it is always the best policy to speak the truth – unless, of course, you are an exceptionally good liar.

'Mummy, have I failed if I only come second?'
Jake, 8

How much you crave success and tolerate failure yourself will undoubtedly affect how you answer Jake here. Hopefully you are a little less judgemental than Bill Shankly, one of Britain's most respected of football managers, who once said, 'If you are first you are first. If you are second, you are nothing.' Not a great message to pass onto your children. As Averil Leimon, a leadership psychologist says, 'I see clients who consistently get to the top in everything they do but never feel a sense of satisfaction. It's just a race because they've been told from such a young age that first is the only position that matters.'

Instead it's important to see both sides, acknowledging that there is nothing wrong with competing and wanting to do your best. But you also need to emphasise that winning isn't the only goal and 'second is the first loser' certainly isn't an adage to be taken to heart. Explaining this while not resorting to trite sporting cliché ('it's not the winning, lad, it's the taking part') will be something of a challenge for any parent.

You could start by championing the status of this much maligned position. 'Look at it the other way, Jake. Second is the next winner not the first loser,' you could say. Emphasise that the point of competing is as much about self-improvement as pitting yourself against others. 'It's the change in your own performance – the base-line as psychologists call it – that really matters and that's what you want to reward as a parent,' says Ros Taylor, business psychologist.

Most importantly, you should be aware of your own ambitions and to what extent you project these onto your own child. 'It's the parental pressure that kills ambition,' says Taylor. 'It's about letting them be good enough. Good enough is fine.'

Leimon agrees. 'That sense of not being desperate to be best but really engaging in something you enjoy is strongly linked with happiness in a lot of psychological research,' she says. You could talk about personal examples where nearly winning has been, hopefully, beneficial in some way. Maybe not achieving the best result in a certain exam, job interview or competition etc allowed you to learn where you were going wrong or resulted in you taking a different route; discovering a new opportunity. 'You need to get across that through failure we can pinpoint our strengths,' says Taylor. 'It's that spirit of, "Let's try again" that is so important.'

Losing – or coming second at least – is likely to increase and develop virtues such as persistence, patience and resilience too. Learning through experience that failure isn't necessarily a catastrophe will improve self-confidence too. As Dr Barry Cripps, a sports psychologist who has researched the nature of competitiveness, winning and losing, says, 'Basically everyone loses more often than they win, it's a bit like gambling; in order to come first in life, you've got to be able to come last – or at least second – too.'

RELATIONSHIP MINEFIELDS

'Mummy, was Daddy the first man you ever kissed?'
Paolo, 7

Somehow it doesn't feel appropriate to give Paolo an illustrious history of his mother's romantic encounters, so should we gloss over the number of frogs Mummy had to kiss before she found his Dad? The best policy is honesty without being too confessional, as in, 'Well, Paolo, how long have you got?'

As Janet Reibstein, therapist and professor of psychology at the University of Exeter, says, 'I'd say "No, your father wasn't the first man I kissed." It's always a bad idea to lie and you want your child to know about how kisses can mean different things to you at different times.'

View Paolo's question as a way into talking about love, affection and how we express these emotions. 'There are kisses you give to Aunt Sophie and good friends,' says Reibstein. Then there are kisses we give to boyfriends and girlfriends when we really like them. 'Introduce the idea that there are developmental stages to kissing. You could say, "Daddy wasn't the first man I kissed but he was the first person where it really meant something. It was different because he was the one I fell in love with and married."'

You could also emphasise to Paolo, if he is in any doubt, that kissing someone you love represents a loving and faithful attachment – especially if you have told him that there were other men you kissed in the past. He may well ask if, in this case, you still kiss other men. 'I think you need to say that now you've met Daddy, he's the only one. That's what a child needs to know,' says psycho-sexual therapist Sarah Fletcher. 'He could be looking for reassurance here and I think it is important to make sure that boundaries are defined; kissing other men was something that happened before Mummy and Daddy got together,' says Fletcher. Although it is also important to mention opposite sex friendship, and how you can kiss a good male friend on the cheek – but it doesn't mean the same thing as kissing Daddy. Just in case there's any possibility of misinterpretation.

Bear in mind that at seven years old, Paolo is growing much more aware of opposite sex relationships and what distinguishes 'kissing' from 'snogging' and friendship from 'fancying'. At this age, boys are already teasing one another about girlfriends and kissing, even though they have little idea of what it may really entail. This curiosity will naturally extend to his own parents, so it's a good chance to talk about how you first met; when you realised you really liked his father and that you didn't want to kiss anyone else. You want to give them a realistic sense that meeting the person you'll stay with for the rest of your life doesn't often happen straight away, which isn't a bad thing at all.

'You need to get across that kissing is what you do when you're getting to know someone,' says Fletcher. 'That it is a necessary part of life, a loving relationship, growing up and finding the right one.'

'Mummy, why were you shouting at each other last night?'
Eloise, 9

It's never pleasant to feel that you've exposed your child to the harsh – yet real – world of adult conflict. In the moment of guilt, don't feel you have to give too much detailed explanation which will make little sense to your child anyway.

What they need at this point is reassurance that they were in no way responsible for the raised voices they overheard and, depending upon the level of acrimony, that Mummy and Daddy still love each other.

Ideally you need to communicate some important truths about arguments while glossing over the minutiae of your particular altercation. You could say that normal arguing – as opposed to bitter and continual fighting – can serve several positive purposes. It can help you to solve problems, negotiate with a partner as well as express feelings in an honest, instinctive way.

'Put the argument into context,' advises Denise Knowles, a family counsellor with Relate. 'Your nine year old doesn't need to know the nitty-gritty. There's no need to burden them in that way. It's important to say that grown-ups do argue but they can also make-up.' Try and introduce examples in their own lives that they can identify with – arguments with siblings and friends and how they can love someone but still not like their point of view or the way they're behaving. You could say that the people we love most – other family members – are the ones we feel most comfortable expressing our true emotions to, and that can include anger. Answering this question confidently and not appearing to be too embarrassed can also reassure them that their own feelings of aggression are normal. If you give your child the impression that adult relationships are only ever harmonious, this could worry a child for different reasons. Susan Quilliam, relationship psychologist and author of *Stop Arguing, Start Talking*, explains, 'A nine year old may want to know that people do feel strongly and it's ok to let your emotions out sometimes – that it's natural as long as it doesn't go too far.' Although bear in mind, too, that we don't want to over-promote the benefits of shouting. 'I think kids need to know they have a range of other ways to cope with genuine conflict,' says Quilliam. So you could bring in other examples where as a family or a couple you have – if possible – agreed on a decision without dispute or raising voices.

At the heart of this question is anger; how you and your partner cope with this emotion and the cues you then give to your children. They will instinctively pick up on their parents attitude to confrontation and you want them to know that it is crucial in all relationships, even if it sometimes means venting emotion. As Quilliam says, 'How to manage those feelings is the issue, not the feelings themselves. It's important to say in so many words, "When we do shout, it's short and sharp – it's simply to let off steam. Then we talk through the issue and in the end we agree – so shouting isn't necessarily a bad thing."' Especially if it can help us reach a constructive conclusion.

'Mummy, Dad is the boss isn't he?'
Hamish, 6

The first question to ask yourself is, quite simply, is it true? Where has Hamish got this idea from and why is he asking it?

Does he feel that Daddy has more authority or that both his parents set the rules when it comes to discipline? 'I'm a big believer that children are shrewd,' says Richard Bailie, child psychologist. 'Maybe it's an idea they've picked up from outside the home but more often than not, it's an issue that will often ring true in some way. It's these kinds of observations from your child that can make you stop and think about your own relationship and behaviour – which is the best starting point.'

Be aware about your response to Hamish's question. Does it upset you? Or do you think it's funny? This will give you some indication as to how accurate Hamish's observation really is. 'If it doesn't bother you, then that's fine,' agrees Bailie. 'If it does, then it's significant.' If it is the latter, save your concern for later and keep your answer cool and neutral. 'I would say, "No-one is the boss in this house – both Mum and Dad are in charge."' Then try and give some examples, advises child development psychologist Elaine Douglas. 'Something like, "Mum looks after the money and what we spend each month and Dad decides what car we buy," if that's the case. You don't want to reinforce the notion that there's a pecking order and the man has a dominating role.'

It is much more likely that Hamish has picked up the idea of Dad being boss from your attitude to discipline and authority. At six years old, this is what will shape his beliefs about parental equality, far more than who does what around the house. So if you're saying, 'No, Hamish you can't do that' but then Dad says 'Yes' and undermines your decision, that's what will influence Hamish's assumptions. 'You have to present a united front,' says Douglas. 'Don't slip into that, "Wait until your father comes home" mentality. Try and deal with issues yourself and don't set up one parent as the authority figure.' Once Hamish senses a lack of cohesion in your attitude to discipline, he may well use it to his advantage – sabotaging one parent to get what he wants from the other. It will also leave him feeling confused – he could well be seeking a genuine answer, rather than trying to test your authority or merely making you slightly paranoid. 'It could be an issue of consistency – the child really wants to know who the boss is,' says Bailie. 'They want to feel contained emotionally.'

This is where the two of you need to set parameters and sit down and talk about what messages you're giving out to Hamish. As Bailie says, 'The bottom line is, what you tell the child will never be as important as what they see.' In an ideal world, that's Mum and Dad sharing responsibility, neither deferring to or undermining one another. Not easy, but the only way you'll really show Hamish who's boss.

'Mummy, why do you always blame Dad when things go wrong?'
Madeleine, 8

Blame is one of the most common relationship ticks that children are exposed to; a lazy reflex that the best of us revert to, often when we're feeling tired, low and frustrated. While we may try and shield our children from a full-blown row, it takes rather more self-restraint to protect them from those low-level gripes that can inform our daily commentary; 'Why does he always leave the milk out? Am I the only one around here who clears up?' 'I can't believe he's taken your sister to the park without her coat.'

Gentle and affectionate jibes about one another's behaviour are fine, within reason, but if Madeleine has noticed enough to comment, it sounds as if this could be something more. The main pitfall of blame is that it's infectious. If one person accuses the other, it's only natural for them to respond defensively – a negative cycle that can easily influence a child's behaviour.

The question itself should prompt you to reflect on how often you do blame your partner – and what type of criticism you're levelling at him. 'I would start by asking them what they mean by blame,' suggests Dr Richard Bailie, a psychologist specialising in children and families. 'Next you could ask them if any particular examples spring to mind. You could say, "When we blame someone we don't really mean everything we say and it can be a way of expressing feelings." But my hunch is that they have hit upon something here and I'd encourage parents to explore the issue between themselves,' he says. 'Do you blame one another for small mistakes? Do you make the other one feel guilty or ashamed about what they've done? It's being able to have a conversation about this sort of pattern,' he says.

Don't worry unduly about how this will affect Madeleine, reassures Bailie. 'See her question as a barometer for what's going on, rather than signifying anything more serious,' he says. Although it could be beneficial to say to her that blame isn't something you're particularly proud of – rather than being defensive. 'There should be a sense of recognition here that it isn't a good thing,' says Sarah Fletcher, psychosexual therapist. 'To say sorry that she's seen it and to admit that sometimes it is easier to blame one's own partner.' As opposed to admitting to your own weakness which is invariably more challenging. 'It is easier to project everything that goes wrong onto someone "out there", rather than looking at your own behaviour, which is a childlike trait and not a healthy way of being – it doesn't lead to any sense of self-awareness,' says Fletcher. The only way to break the cycle is to make a conscious effort to blame yourself instead. There is, as Oscar Wilde once said, 'luxury in self-reproach.' As well as increasing self-awareness, it also makes it a great deal harder for anyone else to blame you either – and that includes children too.

'Mummy, why aren't you married to Daddy – does it mean he doesn't love you?'
Daphne, 8

Blame Cinderella, Sleeping Beauty and every fairytale ending processed by Disney, but there comes a stage when a young girl loves a wedding. When they hit that stage, whether it's three, six, eight or beyond, they want to see pictures of their mother's wedding day, in particular that dress. If those pictures are strangely absent and you are still unmarried, then you've got some explaining to do.

For a girl of Daphne's age, weddings and marriages are the same thing and it is your responsibility to gently point out the yawning difference. 'You could say something like, "Marriage is about a lifelong commitment, working things out day-to-day; it's very different to simply wearing a nice white dress for a few hours"', advises Paula Hall, relationship therapist for Relate. Crucially, you want to emphasise that you don't have to get married to love one another. As Penny Mansfield, director of One-Plus-One, the marriage and partnership research charity, says, 'I'd say, "Not everyone gets married. I love Daddy and Daddy loves me and you don't need to be married to do that."'

The next question is why should Daphne ask this at all? Are her friends talking about their own parents wedding day and teasing her because you don't have a wedding ring? 'If they say, "I'd like you to be married", you need to find out more. Maybe the child is tapping away at something and I'd be led by them – I'd want to know what's going through their head,' says Mansfield. Are there personal issues that she's picking up on; a partner who can't get a divorce or one partner who wants to get married while another is more reluctant, a common reason for couples not to take the final plunge? 'As soon as this question crops up, I think you must reflect yourself on why you aren't married,' advises Mansfield.

'Sometimes one party is more keen to marry than the other and that's tricky to explain. Then you've got to think hard how much you share your personal feelings with your child, giving them insight into an adult relationship which may not be appropriate,' she says. Exclaiming, for example, 'Well, I'd love to marry your father but of course he's scared stiff of the idea,' would be an example of this.

A more familiar reason could be financial which is rather easier to explain. 'That's a reason a lot of couples give,' says Mansfield. 'In research we find that very few people actually say they feel marriage is not a good thing – in the social attitudes survey, those who said they felt marriage was just a bit of paper amounted to less than ten per cent.' Our reasons, it seems, for postponing marriage are more likely to be related to lifestyle considerations. 'One couple I interviewed said, "We were going to get married last year but we thought we'd get a new conservatory first."' Maybe not the best reason to offer Daphne when she pops the question.

'Mummy, why doesn't anyone like me?'
Flora, 7

While most seven-year-old boys are still bounding around like eager puppies, happy to bond with anyone who likes Spiderman, Star Wars or James Bond, the girls are already honing sophisticated social skills; networking and establishing Queen Bee pecking orders.

From the age of seven onwards, girls have an intense social awareness and can be extremely sensitive to perceived slights and put downs. They are already absorbing complex social codes concerned with social acceptance and rejection. Minute acts of disloyalty – such as daring to get along with a girl the rest of the group don't like – can get you ejected from the inner-sanctum quicker than you can say Hannah Montana.

'There are certain conditions to joining in which are difficult to understand to outsiders; it's to do with your interests, tastes and hobbies,' explains Dr Angharad Rudkin, child psychologist specialising in peer problems and relationships. 'It's all about power and social control.'

Which is why they're bound to ask questions like this relatively young – although if and when they do, it's crucial to pinpoint why. First reassure yourself, and Flora, that it is highly unlikely that no-one likes her. Next find out where she has got this idea from, advises Rudkin. 'Has she fallen out with a best-friend? Is it a one-off episode or has it been going on a long time?' If it is an argument, you can remind her that when she's disagreed with friends in the past they have always made up. Talk her through it without jumping to the conclusion yourself that this is a serious problem – you need to help her with a more rational view. Try and reassure her that maybe she has different interests to a certain group she wants to be accepted by.

Another helpful measure is to explore and develop her social skills, suggests Professor Helen Cowie, developmental psychologist specialising in children's relationships. 'Is there something she's doing that's alienating other children? You need to be quite realistic about that. Is their behaviour difficult? Do they find it hard to co-operate?' Research shows that children as young as five years old who are kind, considerate and able to share tend to have closer friendships, and more of them, than those who aren't able to model these social skills.

So it can be very worthwhile to focus on these aspects, talk about the meaning of empathy and praise them when they are generous and caring. It may reassure her – and you – to know that even if she was extremely popular with an extensive network of friends, she wouldn't necessarily be any happier.

In their book *Cliques*, Charlene Giannetti and Margaret Sagarese report that those who aren't in the in-crowd are, on the whole, much more content and secure with a handful of friends, and not so fearful of losing their precarious status. 'Popularity creates constant anxiety,' they write. To maintain that status, you have to please people; behave and maybe dress in a certain way – which brings its own pressures. Flora may not agree, but aiming for Miss Averagely-Popular is a much better place to be.

'Mummy, why doesn't Will's Dad live with him any more?'
Lucas, 8

This is the classic age when children begin to make comparisons, usually unfavourably, with other friends and families, as in, 'Why aren't I allowed to stay up till 10pm like Jack?' Yet this is slightly different – it's less to do with a child's perceived injustice and more to do with potential anxieties about family situations that feel different to their own.

A point to emphasise is that just because a parent isn't physically with a child doesn't mean he doesn't love him. 'You could say there are lots of reasons Will's Daddy isn't there but it's about promoting the idea that even if he isn't in the house, he can still have lots of contact with his son,' says Denise Knowles, a family counsellor for Relate. 'You can draw on your own experiences here. You could say just because Dad goes to work every day or goes away for business doesn't mean he loves you less.'

If Will's parents have separated recently, then it's best not to make too big an issue out of it. 'Don't avoid the subject with Will or his mother but don't behave as if it's the biggest tragedy in the world,' advises Karen Woodall, author of *Putting Children First: A Handbook for Separated Parents.* 'Don't worry if they ask lots of questions either; children often go where we fear to tread; they can be curious about different living arrangements and quite happy to ask about it, which is fine.'

One assumes that single parent families are less beneficial for children than two-parent ones but not necessarily – what impacts a child's well-being is how well the parents get on, whether they are together or apart. 'All of the research we've gathered at the Centre shows that the trouble for children is around high conflict – it's the key aspect that is damaging for them, regardless of whether parents are separated or not,' says Woodall.

Statistically the children who do best in one-parent families are those whose mothers and fathers have successfully managed their differences. Where conflict is low, the relationship between child and separated father is always better.

Which is why you could explain to Lucas that if a parent moves out, often it is for the good of the whole family, not an act of abandonment. Woodall says, 'We always advocate that separating is to help the parents have a relationship with their child that is conflict free; so the time they spend together is good time, not complicated by arguments.' Often it can be reassuring for children in more conventional set-ups to know that people can go through different experiences, like divorce and separation, and adapt well. 'Yes, and children do adjust very well when parents work together,' says Woodall. 'It is also good for any child to know that people can live differently, survive and be ok – it can prepare them for anything unforeseen in the future.'

'Why didn't Charlie invite me to his party?'
Harry, 9

It's a tough challenge but you have to detach yourself from a question so bound to provoke emotions. Protectiveness, anxiety about your child's popularity, resentment at the parent for so callously leaving Harry off the invite list. All these will be magnified if Charlie is a particularly close friend. First try to look for practical reasons why Harry didn't get the call. 'Maybe you've misconstrued it completely and the number had to be limited,' says Professor Helen Cowie, specialising in child development, rather optimistically. 'I would reflect the question back on them,' says educational psychologist Annie Mitchell. 'Ask them why they think they weren't invited – did they do something to upset them? If there's something else going on, then the parent needs to find out.' Has this friend turned against him? Could it be a form of bullying? Chances are this isn't the case but they need to be ruled out.

As well as feeling slighted on your child's behalf, it can feel like a personal rejection too – especially if you happen to know Charlie's mother. You may be as worried about your own social standing and popularity in the school gates' hierarchy as your son's in the playground – in which case you need to get the issue into perspective. 'At this point, you need to step back and think, this is about your child, and not you,' says Mitchell. Sometimes it can be difficult to separate the two; Harry's sense of rejection from your own. Cowie agrees. 'There is a danger that parents can be very competitive about who's invited where.' Of course, it is only natural that you want your child to be popular and included, and to get along with mothers yourself – a parents' sense of positive social belonging is bound to benefit their child's.

In this case, if Harry is very keen on Charlie, maybe you could take a more pro-active stance. 'Another way to get invited next time is to have a party yourself,' says Cowie. 'Don't hang around passively waiting to be included. Ask them for tea or organise a picnic but don't sit at home feeling rejected.' This applies equally to parent and child. 'Be positive and friendly, and if you don't feel included in the in-crowd at the school gates, make friends with other Mums on the fringe. Don't project any of your own inadequacies and anxieties about feeling excluded or snubbed onto your child,' says Cowie.

In fact, chances are your child won't care that much that he hasn't been invited and could be asking the question more out of curiosity than a sense of wounded disappointment. He will, however, be very aware of your response, so try to be upbeat and breezy. 'Say something like, "You don't always get the invite you want; not everyone can go to one party but don't worry, there'll be plenty of other invites and parties in the future,"' says Cowie. If you are thinking, 'That's the last time I bother making small talk with Charlie's Mum at the school pool,' just keep it to yourself.

'Mummy, why are you two talking about money again?' Jake, 7

Forget sex, drugs and alcohol, this is often the more sensitive topic. Our relationship with money is uniquely emotional, subjective, anxious and fraught, particularly in these uncertain times.

Jake will pick all this up in due course, all the more reason to present a pragmatic, rather than an emotional, attitude towards finance and money. It can be an emotionally loaded topic and children will sense this, agrees Professor Karen Pine, developmental psychologist and author of *Sheconomics*, a financial guide for women. The first point is to keep it neutral. Discuss money openly and sensibly but it shouldn't be a topic that's argued about or loaded with emotion.

So try to be matter of fact in your explanation. 'I would say something like, "Mum and Dad are talking about money so we can sort out some household payments. It's something we do regularly together so we can come to an agreement and it's fine,"' says Pine. 'If they can see you negotiating and handling finance in a positive way then its a good role model for them.' Although the actual value of money is still a relatively abstract concept to most seven year olds, it's power and allure will be less so – they'll be increasingly curious about where it comes from and how to get hold of it. Ideally we should inform and educate them about money without giving away too many details over which they have no power.

So, a simple discussion about what happens to the economy when banks and households borrow too much is fine. What you should avoid is personalising the situation as in, 'We can't afford x, y, z because our mortgage payment has gone up – Lord only knows how we'll afford it.' 'It's not right to involve them in this way or expect them to understand,' says Pine. 'It can be frightening to a child to say, "We may not have any money at the end of this month."'

Also avoid associating money with terms like comfort or security because the obverse to that will be 'less money equals less security' which isn't a message you necessarily want to give out, she advises. Nor is it particularly healthy to imply our emotional security and well-being is dependent on large amounts of dosh. This can be easier said than done when our attitude towards money is so subtly linked with self-worth. As psychotherapist Sue Cowan-Jenssen says, 'People can think, "If I have enough money, I'll be special, or people won't look down on me." We think it will buy us self-worth. Children can pick this up from their family and from our culture too.'

Hopefully Jake is simply inquisitive about money, rather

than absorbing our own particular hang-ups. His question could be a good opportunity to talk about practical tips and the benefits of saving. 'Encouraging them to put 20p aside each week can teach them about delaying gratification,' suggests Pine. 'You can also involve him in purchasing decisions – showing him how we shop around for the best-value options.'

Who knows, he may even avoid the mistakes of his parents credit-happy generation and learn to save instead.

WHY DID MUM AND DAD DO THAT?

'Mummy, why did you give me such a weird name?'
Alabama, 8

Good point, Alabama. It could be a reminder of where
Alabama's mother and father fell in love or even conceived their
precious progeny. There are two possible reasons why she
may be asking such a question and you'll know which one it
is by the tone of her voice. Was it one of lively curiosity or did
it contain that unmistakable accusing edge with the emphasis
on *did*? Either way, you need to be honest and positive in
your response, advises Gaynor Sbuttoni, educational psychologist. 'They may not like the name and if that's the case then
you need to acknowledge that and say, "OK. That's your taste."
You also need to say something like, "I love your name and
I needed a name to go with the baby I loved which is why I
chose it."'

Dr Nadja Reissland, developmental psychologist at Durham
University, adds. 'Tell them why you chose their name; a book
you read, a film or a family name. If it is, for example, Louis –
tell him about King Louis; the palaces and castles, the history.
In this way, they can feel more positive and start to own the
name rather than feeling it's been given to them for no reason

If Alabama is being teased or picked on at school because of her name then, says Sbuttoni, you need to sit down and work out some coping strategies. 'You could suggest how she responds to her friends – could she say something like, "I don't care if you don't like my name. I like it so it's your problem." Anything to nullify the comment and show them that she isn't a victim. You could even role play with her and rehearse how she'd act when she next gets teased.'

It's important to encourage Alabama to have confidence in her own name. As Reissland says, 'Part of that comes from teaching your child how to shrug off the jokes, laughing along with it – or even pre-empting it.'

There is also no point blaming yourself, as a parent, for a name that years later draws ridicule. Louis, for example, is a faultless name until your five year old comes home from school and accuses you of making his life a misery because friends teasingly call him 'Pooey Louis'. When parents are considering names, it is impossible to predict just how ingenious their friends will be, making mockery of your best intentions. As Sbuttoni says, 'You can try and think, "I won't call them that because someone's bound to rhyme it with this" but you can't second guess. It's better to pick a name you like and focus on giving your children the skills to deal with it. Humour, in particular, is probably the best way to win friends around to an unusual name. As in, "My Mum loved Alabama when she stayed there with my Dad, thank goodness it wasn't Basingstoke or Bangor."'

'Mummy, why do you shave your legs?'
Ruby, 7

A little honesty combined with a sprinkling of history is the best way forward with this question. Take a few seconds to reflect why, really, you do shave your legs. Since there's no practical reason, the unavoidable truth is it's very much concerned with Mummy's vanity and appearance, not that there's anything wrong with that. You could say that there's something satisfying about shearing away unsightly bristles and exposing a gleaming satin-skinned leg underneath.

You could also explain to Ruby that shaving one's legs is a convention dictated to women but one which we don't necessarily have to follow. You don't want her to assume it's something women *have* to do in order to be accepted and valued. I would say to her, "You can choose not to shave your legs. It makes me feel better but you may not feel the same way,"and that would be sufficient,' says Dr Dana Wilson-Kovacs, lecturing in sociology, gender and sexuality at the University of Exeter.

Doctor Lizzy Dark, educational psychologist, agrees, 'I would respond by saying that it's something women can choose to do when they're grown up if they want to. It would be important to stress that it's every woman's choice what they do with their bodies – whether or not it's what other people say they should do.'

It may help Ruby to understand this apparently strange ritual if you offer her some context. 'It's a nice way of introducing some history on the subject,' agrees Wilson-Kovacs who explains, 'If you look at art history, you'll find that not only leg hair but all body hair from the Renaissance upto the 20th century is restricted to the head which is to do with traditional Western forms of femininity. There is an unspoken norm that body hair shouldn't be shown.'

In more recent history, you could say, women's legs have been more exposed since fashion dictated a rise in hemlines in the 1920s – around this time they started marketing the first female safety razor. World War II had a particular impact; nylons were rationed and women had to wear bare legs to save money. In desperation they drew lines up the back of them to look like stockings, so their legs had to look even smoother. In the 1970s, body hair became a political issue and Germaine Greer condemned it in *The Female Eunuch* as a betrayal of true 'femaleness'. Although what she failed to do is advise mothers what to tell their daughters on the subject. Wilson-Kovacs agrees, 'Unfortunately feminists haven't left a body of work on how to deal with this question.'

Presumably because they would never be caught shaving their legs by their daughters – or sons – in the first place. These days it's rather less clear cut. Now the UK hair-removal market is worth £280 million a year, and 92% of us admit to shaving our legs. That includes feminists too, presumably. So we enjoy gender equality but we also like smooth legs, a conflict that young Ruby, like her mother, will somehow have to resolve.

'Mummy, why do you have to go to work?'
Pheobe, 8

Or to re-phrase this in terms more familiar to many working mothers, 'Mum, do you *have* to go to work?', pitched in a suitably plaintive, guilt-inducing tone just as you reach the front door. 'Yes I do, how else could we afford (delete as necessary) piano lessons, pony club, birthday trip to Euro Disney, and a second car for the au pair?' Which is, of course, the wrong answer.

'If you say I have to go out to work to pay for your stuff, it instantly throws the guilt straight back to your child,' says Denise Taylor, author of *Working Mothers – The Essential Guide*. 'You could say words to the effect, "I have ambitions which is why I enjoy work but it also means I can be a better mother and we can enjoy the times we have together much more." It's important to let them know that work – your time away – doesn't detract from your relationship with them.'

If you really feel that it doesn't impact negatively, it's unlikely they will either. Either way this is one of those perceptive questions that should prompt you to reflect a little further. 'Why, indeed, do you go to work?' Is it purely to pay the bills; would you go to work if you didn't need the money? Would you prefer to spend more time with your children? 'Questions like this can be a wake up call,' says relationships psychologist Susan Quilliam. It's also worth remembering that a child will be more likely to ask such a question if they sense any negativity you have about your job. Fine to admit that sometimes we have our off days – just as they do when they think about going back to school on a Monday morning.

As a working mother, ideally, you want to be able to convey to Pheobe that a good job is, and should be, as much about personal fulfilment as financial independence – and that one doesn't necessarily equal the other. Quilliam agrees, 'The first point to get across is that work is necessary and it can be enjoyable too. You want to give your daughter a sense that a career is useful and essential and that she can control her life through the medium of work. Think what message you want to give to your child about independence, money and fulfilment.'

Or you can assure them that happier mothers make for happier children and then quote this salient research; according to a report from the Institute of Social and Economic Research (at the end of last year), working mothers are far more content than those that stay at home. Even mothers who work more than 45 hours a week reported significantly higher levels of satisfaction than those full-time mothers who spend their hours baking fairy cakes and getting inventive with Play Dough. Repeating this may not impress an eight year old significantly, but it may make you feel better.

'Mummy, why do you find that funny?'
Ned, 7

If you're *really* laughing, as opposed to politely amused, there's very little chance you'll admit to your seven-year-old son why – the funniest jokes are usually inappropriate by definition. This is because, like children, we're drawn to taboos. We're hard-wired to laugh at the stuff we feel we shouldn't which, of course, makes it virtually impossible – if it's a good adult joke – to tell Ned the real source of your mirth.

'Death and sex are the topics we find funny because we know we're not supposed to,' explains Richard Wiseman, psychology professor, who set out to find the world's funniest joke. (If you're wondering, the best visual joke was the scene where Del Boy falls off a pub bar).

'It's the same for children,' says Wiseman. 'It's just they've got different taboos. So they wouldn't understand your joke anyway.' Which is why Ned, like most seven year olds, will find any mention of poo hilarious. Meanwhile you're left wondering when their puerile humour will become more sophisticated, enabling them to appreciate the comic subtlety of a man falling off the end of a pub bar.

This is one of the few areas where experts agree that a white lie wouldn't go amiss. 'Depending on what it's about, it's a no-brainer – we have a duty to protect our kids. But we also have to pitch our explanation to their level,' says Doctor Chris Arnall, a psychologist who specialises in stress management and humour. 'You could use an example from your child's life to make it easier to explain why you're laughing ie. Do you remember that time when your friend had spaghetti on his face..' Wiseman suggests distraction as one option. 'By the time you've explained any joke, you've killed it dead. So, you could say, "Well, this was funny in the same way that this is funny," and tell them a joke so they don't feel left out. Humour is a bonding thing and you want to elicit joint laughter.'

To achieve that rarity it helps to understand what your child laughs at and why. According to Jean Piaget, the pioneering Swiss developmental psychologist, children's humour is a crucial aspect of their emotional growth. He discovered that they really only understand jokes from around ten years and beyond; it takes them this long to grasp the concept of empathy – being able to see other points of view and appreciate different worlds from their own. 'It's abstract thinking,' says Arnall.

'The ability to go beyond the known and the concrete.'

Until then, the next best thing are those films and cartoons that offer the illusion of 'shared humour'. 'The perfect situation is where parents and children are laughing at different levels of the same joke so everyone feels included,' says Wiseman. Perhaps the best solution is to sit down and watch *The Simpsons*; Ned can giggle at Homer falling over, while you laugh knowingly when he says, 'All right brain. You don't like me and I don't like you, but lets just do this and I can get back to killing you with beer.' No explanation needed.

'Why did Daddy shout *that* word when we were in the car?'
Keenan, 6

If it's the first time that six-year-old Keenan has witnessed a raised voice and a profanity in the car, then Daddy is something of a saint, or maybe Mummy is just a genius at map reading. Or Daddy's language is even more florid than usual. Either way, you've got some explaining to do.

We know instinctively that children will imitate our speech and as responsible parents we should set an example, but it's not always that easy. First, how to explain the expletive itself. If Keenan starts to chant it from the back seat, then the most effective strategy is to pretend that it's one of Dad's silly, made-up words, however horrifying the 'bad' word in question may sound from the mouth of an innocent six year old. This can be an endurance test in itself.

'I wouldn't draw attention to the word,' says educational psychologist Doctor Lizzy Dark. 'You shouldn't overreact and attach more importance to it than it deserves.' Overreacting when you hear Keenan repeat it is like handing him a grenade he can detonate at any time, most probably in front of guests and in-laws. Your challenge is to neutralise its capability with feigned, placid indifference.

You can remind yourself that swear words aren't inherently offensive, anyway. Society decides what we view as profane or otherwise, according to Tony McEnery, professor of linguistics at Lancaster University and author of *Swearing in English. Bad Language, Purity and Power from 1586 to the Present*. 'Words also shift in their acceptability and unacceptability over time – "My God" isn't viewed as badly as it used to be; other racist terms now are seen as much worse, especially among younger people. Language use changes all the time.'

It's also useful to bear in mind that there are points in a child's development when they'll be a lot more aware of what is socially taboo and what isn't – which is what gives those words their allure. The first time is during nursery and early primary school when children find anything to do with excretion numbingly hilarious – this can last for many years and even as adults we're not immune. The second is early adolescence when coarser language is part of peer culture, so they'll be imitating their friends and not you.

Meanwhile, if Keenan doesn't copy Dad's swear word and is just more upset at the idea that he lost his temper, then it's best to be honest and explain that sometimes we all get cross and say words that don't sound very nice. This could also be an opportunity for a more general discussion, advises Dark. 'It's a good point to sit down as a family and decide what is acceptable and unacceptable language.' Which is an effective way of setting boundaries for yourself, as well as your children. 'You could think of substitutes for both parents and children to stick to; like "gosh" or "golly" (or if that's a bit Enid Blyton, "blast" is another alternative) instead of "God", or "be quiet" instead of "shut up", and as soon as they use the appropriate word, jump on that chance to praise them,' says Dark. And praise Dad too if he manages a zen-like, "Be quiet, please", the next time you're lost off the Hanger Lane gyratory and Keenan is screaming for the loo – God knows he'd deserve it.

'Mummy, why are you two so embarrassing?' Nathan, 15

Embrace one simple truth; however you behave, Nathan will always, or for the duration of his adolescence at least, view you as terminally uncool.

Never mind that you have bought the Kings of Leon album, a new iPhone and you're an avid fan of *The Wire*, this will count for nothing in the eyes of a cruelly judgemental teen. Rather than taking it personally, reassure yourself it is a natural and healthy part of their development. 'If I meet fathers and sons or mothers and daughters who are similar; who wear similar clothes and say similar things, I worry about them,' says Dr Rachel Andrew, a psychologist specialising in family issues. 'That they find you embarrassing means they're starting to form their own identity, have their own beliefs. It's a way of saying, "You're so different from me", and that's a positive sign.' If not a crushing one, but reassure yourself that it's a pretty universal accusation – remember how intensely embarrassing your parents could be? 'This sentiment is so widespread,' says Andrew. 'I always say to parents, treat it as a bit of a joke and be quite light-hearted about it. Don't be defensive.'

If you're brave enough, you could always ask Nathan exactly why he finds you so embarrassing. 'It would be helpful to find out the impact of whatever it is that's embarrassing them,' agrees Richard Bailie, a child psychologist. 'Maybe it's because you're making them do something that's different to their other friends, like coming home much earlier in the evening. It's worth finding out and seeing if it's something you can negotiate,' he says.

Rather than making one trite quip and closing the conversation, try and open up a discussion. 'Firstly, I would try and normalise what they're feeling,' says Bailie. 'Talk about how and why you found your parents embarrassing and any other examples you can think of to show they're not the only person in that situation.'

Also be aware of why they may have raised the issue. Are they feeling particularly sensitive about not fitting in with their peers? 'Remember that from 12 years old onwards, friends are everything,' says Bailie. 'They are terrified of being rejected and being accepted by their group is crucial to their identity. All these emotions are very raw to them.' Ideally you should acknowledge their embarrassment; not take their slights too seriously and yet be sensitive to their emotions – and you thought it was tricky negotiating with toddlers.

'Teenagers are really clever at knowing what buttons to push and will often use this one as a bargaining tool,' warns Andrew. As in, 'You're so embarrassing –why can't you let me stay out at x's, buy x or wear x, like my friends easy-going parents?' At this point, stand firm and don't believe they'll stop calling you embarrassing if you give in this once – they'll find plenty of other opportunities to tell you that you're naff and obselete. 'It's important not to get hung up that so-and-so's parent is so much cooler for whatever reason,' says Bailie. 'Decide how to steer the ship and don't be blown off course.'

'Mummy, why don't I ever see Daddy cry?'
Freddie, 7

This question immediately begs another – why, one wonders, is Freddie asking such a question right now? Is it that he has seen his mother cry more publicly in recent times than his father? Is he curious if one parent is expressing their emotions in a more open way than the other?

On a less personal level, Freddie's query is concerned with gender and social conditioning – an area that will impact him increasingly beyond the age of seven. So you could start with his own experiences; has he noticed girls of his age crying more than boys? If so, why does he think this could be? Does he feel comfortable crying? If not, why?

Crying is only natural, after all – a purely physiological

function which you can illustrate to Freddie by talking about the three types of tears that we tend to cry. 'Basal tears lubricate the eyes,' explains Dr Simon Moore, an academic leader in psychology who has also researched the function of crying. 'Reflex tears are a physical response to wash out irritants like, say, peeling onions. Then, of course, emotional tears which have been found to contain higher levels of a hormone manganese – some people say this substance helps to relieve stress.'

At which point you can emphasise the merits of emotional crying. 'One fact we know is that positive hormones are released when we cry,' says Moore. 'People often feel much more positive after they've shed some tears. I would say, we have tear ducts and they are there for good reason. We're physically designed to cry so why shouldn't we?'

The primary reason is social conditioning. You could talk here about the different ways that girls and boys are encouraged to show their emotions. Boys are still encouraged from a young age to appear, on the outside at least, tough, independent, aggressive and resilient in front of others. As Dr Joan Harvey, a senior lecturer in psychology at Newcastle University, says, 'There is ample evidence that even from a young age boy babies are treated differently to girl babies – they handled more abrasively. We reinforce our expectations continually with the message that they should be "Big brave boys".' Their favourite heroes – from Batman to Bond – would tend to reinforce this overall sense that crying represents weakness.

So as boys reach adolescence, we shouldn't be surprised that there is a marked increase in boys crying much less than girls.

By the time they reach 18 years old, women will cry on average four times more than men. That works out at about 5.3 cries a month compared to a man's 1.4 a month, according to research carried out by Dr William Frey, an American biochemist who is a leading expert in tear research. You could say that these facts explain why men, including Daddy, are still less likely to cry in public than women.

But times are changing, you could stress, and it is now viewed as beneficial and positive if men can express their feelings more openly. At which point you may want to include Dad in the discussion. When, indeed, was the last time he cried? Hopefully he'll admit that, on occasion, he can feel emotionally moved to tears – like the last time the English rugby team won the world cup.

If Freddie's Dad is looking for a swift way out, he could impress his son with American author Kurt Vonnegut's thoughts on the subject: "I myself prefer to laugh, since there is less cleaning up to do afterwards."

'Why are you nagging me to eat up, when you're always on a diet?
Flora, 10

Children are highly aware of our sometimes complex attitude towards food. Even if you don't recognise any mixed messages – like trying to restrain your own appetite while encouraging Flora's – she certainly will. Any inconsistency and contradiction – particularly where diets are concerned – will be picked up on. Crucially, if you are on a diet, pay close attention to how you talk about it in front of your child. 'You could say, "Right now, I'm not as healthy as a I could be and I'm trying to eat more sensibly." But don't say you're on a diet to lose weight,' advises psychotherapist Linda Blair.

'You need to really look out for the language you use when you discuss eating and food – whether you tend towards words like "fattening", "slimming" or "good for you" and "enjoyable",' says Blair. The latter being preferable. Watch out too for the words you use when you talk about yourself. Be aware of those moments when you catch yourself in the mirror and want to say, or even do say, in dismay, 'God, I look like a melted candle from the waist down', while your daughter watches on, soaking up the jaded self-criticism like a sponge.

Be mindful of branding certain foods as 'good' or 'bad', as in, 'Aren't you lucky you can eat chocolate, dear, while poor old Mummy has to stick to boring salads'. 'I've done a lot of work on the communication between mothers and daughters between nine to 11 years old,' says psychology professor Andrew Hill, specialising in nutrition, eating disorders and obesity. 'Parents just aren't as aware as their children of their own behaviour. They don't realise that kids are so sensitive to how parents feel about their own appearance, especially at a time when they're looking forward to being adults.'

Parents can also be unaware of the more subtle ways their food insecurities can play out through their children. It could be that Flora is somehow integral to her mother's dieting regime – which isn't uncommon. 'There is evidence that mothers on diets can use their children as dustbins; gaining vicarious pleasure from watching a child eating cake or chips,' says Professor Jane Ogden, author of *The Psychology of Eating*. 'One study I was involved in showed that dieters can make less healthy choices for their children; often using them to clear food away because it stops the temptation. Dieting mothers are often trying to manage the environment; encouraging children to eat up so food is less available for them.'

The litmus test is how family-friendly is Flora's diet? If it's unrealistically low-calorie or high-protein, it can't be that well-balanced and suitable for children. As Hill says, 'If you want to eat healthily, the best approach to bear in mind is; food is part of life and whatever you eat is part of the family menu.'

'Mummy, how come Daddy never uses the washing machine?'
Maria, 9

'Yes darling, and he finds it just as difficult to switch on the hoover and locate the iron,' you may want to add in barbed tones. Whether you work or you're a full-time mother, housework will, at some stage or another, be a contentious issue.

'Chore wars', as they've come to be known, are all the more messy if they haven't been resolved by the time children come along. To give Maria a fair and honest answer, much will depend on how well you've discussed and agreed amicably who does what in the household.

If you've happily carved out traditional roles where Daddy is out working and you're at home, then it's a pretty straightforward answer. You could say, 'We both share our duties in different ways; Daddy earns money so we can live well and I look after you and do the cleaning which is just as important. We play to our strengths but we're both doing the same amount of work.' Or you could be a little less rosy but more realistic and say that, even in these supposed enlightened times, women still end up doing rather more around the house than they probably want to. The latest Time Use Survey by the Office for National Statistics shows that women do 178 minutes of housework a week compared with 100 by men. Marriage, it seems, really does change everything – a report last year from the Royal Economic Society reported that married women spend on average 15 hours a week cooking and cleaning compared with only five hours a week for married men.

You need to consider what messages you want to give to Maria. How happy do you feel about the examples you're setting her? Would you mind if she was ironing her husband's shirts in 30 years time, or would you prefer it if she shared the load? As Dr Katherine Rake, director of the Fawcett Society, which campaigns for equality between men and women, says, 'It's hugely important to be aware of the signals we're sending to children. If we want roles to change, we have to give them a real sense of equal role models.'

But to do that we have to lay the groundwork first. 'You need to have a policy that's been discussed between the two of you,' says Christine Northam, a relationship counsellor for Relate. What you don't want to end up doing is saying something negative in response, like, 'Dad doesn't use the hoover because he's so lazy, so I have to do it.'

Or you could use Maria's question as a way into setting new rules with your partner. 'This sort of query can often be a trigger for a couple to talk about their roles and agree on who does what. Housework is only a problem when a couple hasn't sat down to talk about it,' says Northam.

Maybe there's no harm in reminding Maria of that old-fashioned saying, 'I like hugs, I like kisses but what I love is help with the dishes.'

'Mummy, why don't you like my new friend?'
James, 7

If your child is even asking this, you have to question what sort of signals you've been sending out – and why? Whatever the reason, they can't be that subtle if a seven year old senses such ambivalence. Perhaps you worry about his influence on James when they're together; maybe they talk too much in class or fight in the playground? But are your objections about James's friend really fair? Is he really that much of a bad influence, or is this more to do with your own prejudices?

'Is it the way they talk or dress? Is it their class? Be aware of these blind spots before you sit down and start telling your child what to do,' says child psychologist Dr Angharad Rudkin. Once you've decided that your reservations are valid and you're not a hopeless snob who wants James to mix exclusively with the class A-list (come on, own up), then try and be open with him without sounding too critical. There's no point trying to deny that you're worried about the friendship either, advises

Rudkin. 'Depending on his age, you could say something like, "Sometimes I think he does things/behaves in ways that aren't very nice and I feel you may behave like that too."Or, "Sometimes I wonder why he doesn't always include you and just makes you feel left out."'

Try to be clear on what sort of changes you'd like to see to be happy with the friendship. Set clear targets for him. 'If it's a serious concern, you could ask James to prove himself first with the reward of doing something nice together ie, "If you can show me that you can be friends without fighting/talking in class etc, then the three of us could go somewhere for a treat,"' suggests Dr Rachel Andrew, a psychologist specialising in family issues.

Offer positive incentive and don't be too judgemental – remember that the more objections you raise, the more exciting the friendship may seem. 'If you stand in the way, the more resistant your child may become,' says Dr Andrew. If you do want to seize some control, then do so in a way that doesn't come across as overbearing. 'You could try and encourage other friendships by asking other children to the house. It's being slightly strategic but it can often help them to change or add to their friendships,' says Rudkin.

Ideally, unless you really fear for the safety or happiness of your child, you should keep your distance and let your child make their own decisions. Once children sense parental disapproval about their choices in life, they'll be less likely to feel they can come to you for objective advice when they really need it. So be encouraging and realistic – as Andrew says, 'Reassure yourself that friendships at this age are often short-lived. And if James isn't being treated well, he'll soon move on.'

'Mummy, why won't Dad ever let me win at Monopoly? Jacob, 8

There are two schools of thought when it comes to playing games with our children. Competitive Dad would say, 'The world is a harsh place and the sooner Jacob learns there are always going to people out there who want to beat him, the better. It's the only way he'll improve his game.' Non-competitive Dad would argue that it's much better to let him win, enabling him to build confidence and not feel too hopeless and inferior in comparison to his father.

Many parents, except Jacob's Dad it seems, are only too aware of our children's sensitivity to losing and wonder to what extent we should shield them from the possibility of failure. The key, according to Jill Bellinson, psychotherapist and author of *Children's Use of Boardgames in Psychotherapy*, is to combine both schools of thought. Follow Competitive Dad's example and play at your own level – don't feel you have to let them win simply to protect their delicate egos. But don't be too rigid about the rules either.

'They can learn a great deal if the adult plays as best he or she can, allowing the child to play how they want, turning a blind eye if they miscount squares etc,' says Bellinson. In other words, give them what they need to get ahead and to feel like they're competing equally with you.

All those classic family games – like Monopoly, Connect 4 and Pictionary – can often stir up competitiveness between parents and children, as well as between mother and father, and siblings. What can be surprising is the intense desire of both parents and children to win, and to what extent we often take the game rather more seriously than it merits.

'I have even been taken aback by my own three daughters' levels of competitiveness when we used to sit down to play boardgames,' admits Dr Barry Cripps, a sports psychologist who has researched competitiveness, in particular our attitudes towards winning and losing. But he is keen to stress that we shouldn't view such naked ambition as a negative trait. 'If it can come to the fore in this situation it is a good thing. It is about facing up to and confronting our competitive spirit, and enjoying it.'

Although Competitive Dad shouldn't take this as a green light to pursue his own personal desire to win above all else. 'Some Dads imagine it's a good way to teach their children the value of losing but really it's always best to be aware of your children's needs above your own wish to win,' says Bellinson.

Also reassure yourself that losing in a boardgame can teach Jacob valuable lessons. 'Being able to tolerate rules, learning not to get too upset, coping with frustration when luck doesn't go your way – these are major developmental issues that children have to face up to outside the game as well as in it,' says Bellinson. Maybe Jacob's Dad needs to face up to them too.

WHAT A WEIRD WORLD

'Mummy, why is that man sleeping on the street?'
Amaya, 8

This is the perfect example of the way children can so often see what we choose to stop seeing, and to ask questions that we've simply learnt to ignore. 'What's interesting is when you talk to a nine year old about homelessness, they have a simple moral vision and can see how unfair it is, and how that unfairness shouldn't be tolerated,' says Adam Sampson, chief executive of Shelter.

Even if some of the explanations may not be that easy or pleasant, you should at least try to be candid with Amaya, advises Sampson. 'When my son asks about my job, I say I try to help people find a house but it can be tough for them. Often they can have experienced particular problems and personal tragedies. Drugs and alcohol are often an issue. A lot of people will have come out of places like prison and the army where they've never been able to hold onto a home. I say it is also difficult because there aren't enough houses in the country; even if everyone was perfectly behaved, they would still lose out.'

Injustice is a tough reality to present to a child but it can also help to develop a sense of altruism as well as a world beyond their own. Averil Leimon, leadership psychologist agrees. 'I would want to have as honest a discussion as I could about trying to imagine the circumstances that could lead to someone being on the streets. I would certainly touch on drink and drugs and how people get into bad habits. I would reflect with them on what it must be like leading that kind of life; maybe they were ill. Maybe they've suffered from mental illness. Since one in four people will have mental health problems of some sort, I think it's realistic to talk about people feeling vulnerable.'

It is also a good opportunity to look at morals and personal values. 'You could ask what kind of responsibility do we think we have to help these people? In comparison we are so fortunate, so what do we think is the right thing to do here? It's that kind of dialogue I would encourage,' says Leimon.

Children at around eight years old are at an ideal age to understand the importance of home and needing one's own space – and what the opposite could feel like. 'My nine year old's bedroom is the centre of his universe,' says Samson. 'It's his home, his little world. When I talk to him about the huge number of children who don't have that; who maybe sleep on a sofa or a corridor, suddenly the penny drops and, again, he can understand how unfair it is.'

Inevitably the skill with this question is striking a middle ground; not weighing children down with society's ills, or letting them feel guilty for enjoying the comforts of home, but simply acknowledging that other childrens' lives can be so different – unfairly different – from their own.

'Mummy, why should I keep my clothes on?'
Esme, 4

At a certain age, children love nothing more than to peel their clothes off and you can see why. Clothes can feel restricting, socially and physically, and somehow it's more fun without them. When children take them off, they often behave in a wilder less inhibited way. 'In many ways it's fine for them to run around with nothing on – to let them appreciate that sense of freedom, it's not unhealthy to enjoy that feeling,' says educational psychologist Gaynor Sbuttoni. As long as there are certain boundaries – in and outside the home. 'It's all about teaching them that time and place is important,' she says.

In a supermarket or any communal space you don't feel happy about, a practical response is best – and truthful too. 'I would say, "No you can't take them off because you'll get cold and everyone wears clothes; that's the rule and that's what we do", and leave it at that,' says child psychologist Ruth Coppard. If that feels a little brief, you could give an example that will feel more familiar to them, suggests Sbuttoni: 'As in, when you're in a small shop you can't run around but when you're in a field you can – some places are suitable to do certain things in but others aren't and it's the same when it comes to keeping your clothes on.'

If Esme asks the question more out of general curiosity, then you could match her question with another to gauge her thoughts on the subject. 'I would turn it back on her and ask, "Why do you think you have to keep your clothes on?"', suggests Sbuttoni. 'Encourage them to think of the answers themselves and run through possible reasons: they keep us warm, they protect our skin.' It's also a good opportunity to discuss the notion of public and private – that it feels ok to behave in certain ways in the privacy of our home but not in front of other people. 'It's fine to say that keeping our clothes on is about being private; that there are some things we're happier doing on our own, such as going to the toilet, because it feels more comfortable.'

Naturists would say that taking our clothes off is the ultimate comfort – weather permitting. Andrew Welch, commercial manager for British Naturism, explains, 'The point is we were all born naked. Weather, fashion and convention may dictate that clothes are necessary but we shouldn't lose sight of the fact that they're not as essential as you think.' Welch also believes prudery isn't healthy for children. 'The taboo of nakedness can cause them more problems as they reach puberty – a lot of teenage hang-ups are down to maintaining this mystery of the human body when there shouldn't be any at all.'

Welch is right that our own attitudes will undoubtedly affect our offspring. 'How we handle our own dressing and undressing will play its part,' agrees Sbuttoni. Ideally we want to convey to our children, in an age of cosmetic surgery and idealised images, that we feel comfortable with our bodies. As Sbuttoni says, 'What we're aiming for is not feeling embarrassed about nudity on the one hand but not parading around too much on the other – that's what will provide them with a good role model.'

'Mummy, why do people smoke when they know it could kill them?'
Jason, 10

Faced with the indisputable logic of Jason's question, it is even tougher to admit you may once have been – or still are – one of those people who pursued a pleasure even though it is harmful.

As a parent, do you come clean? And is it really appropriate to shatter Jason's rationale with an introduction to the nature of pleasure and addiction? The answer, according to experts is yes, with some careful editing.

Don't shy away from admitting to human weakness – your own or anyone else's – since any definition of addiction will require it. Reassure yourself that you're much more likely to offer Jason more accurate and insightful comments if you have had first-hand experience. 'I think it's fine to say, if you did smoke, something like, "It's a very stupid thing to do but it's really hard to stop. I wish I'd listened to my Mummy and Daddy. But you can be really clever and not do what I did",' says child psychologist Ruth Coppard.

They may then ask, what makes it so dificult to give up? 'You could say it's an addiction; the feeling that you simply can't do without that drug,' says David Balfour, professor of behavioural pharmocology at the Univeristy of Dundee. 'It's important to get across to a child that it is extremely difficult to give up: on average it takes five or six attempts to quit success- fully. You also need them to understand that this is a good reason for not experimenting because it's so easy to become addicted.' Which offers a slight get-out clause, ie. it's not because people are weak that they continue to smoke but rather because the drug is so powerful.

You could also add without sounding entirely reckless and irresponsible, that it's not that accurate to say *all* people who smoke will die. 'They need to know that it's not a terrible thing but that it's not desirable thing either. You can say that it's cer- tainly not good for your health and every adult should be doing everything they can to give up. But I'd explain that it's not as black and white as they may think,' says psychologist Dr Jeremy Adams who specialises in behavioural aspects of addiction. After all, if they discover that smoking doesn't kill everyone, they may assume it's not such a bad habit after all.

Adams also suggests an analogy. 'You could ask them to imagine they're really hungry and someone says they can have a piece of chocolate now, or wait half an hour and have two chunks, and ask them how they'd feel. Multiply that by a hundred and that's pretty much what a grown-up feels when they're addicted to smoking.'

Most smokers, especially if they are parents, would love to give up, you can tell Jason, but it's not that easy. On a positive note many do and will find the willpower to avoid smoking altogether or give up. Eventually the disadvantages of smoking far outweigh any short-term pleasure, you can say.

As Coppard says, 'I think it's good for children to understand that adults have battles too.' If you're no longer smoking, you can smugly say we usually win them too.

'Mummy, why can't I trust strangers?'
Lila, 6

It is a shame if young Lila already feels that she can't trust people she doesn't know. This question demands a tricky balancing act; wanting our children to be sensible without making them feel fearful. We need our children to believe in the goodwill of strangers; we don't want them to grow up feeling mistrustful and anxious of adults yet instinctively we want to protect them from perceived risks, however slim they may be. So how to steer a middle course?

'I think it's best to avoid the word "stranger",' advises Eileen Hayes, parenting advisor for the NSPCC. 'You can't have a blanket rule of never talking to strangers,' she says. 'It would be more helpful to say, "You mustn't talk to someone you don't know without asking me."'

The 'stranger danger' approach that originated from America in the 1970s is something many childcare experts are less enthusiastic about now. 'I know that the NSPCC has avoided those terms because they don't feel they're helpful,' says Hayes who believes strongly that you should show children who it's ok to talk to by example – in this way, they will absorb your sense of judgement and style of sociability. 'It's about them seeing who it's fine to talk to; the postman, the woman in the post office etc. If, say, someone strange came up and you backed away, you'd say, "Mummy didn't feel comfortable talking to that person." They pick it up from your behaviour,' says Hayes.

Even so, you may want to establish some boundaries, especially if you feel Lila is particularly extrovert or impulsive. As educational psychologist Mallory Henson says, 'Young children are vulnerable and there is the worry they will act on impulse. They don't necessarily think through consequences and, certainly at six years old, they don't have the reasoning and reflection skills of an adult.' Henson advises starting on a positive note, opening the question up for discussion and talking about adults that it is ok to trust. 'People you know, people who work in shops, libraries etc. Then you can say you wouldn't get into a car with an adult you didn't know, or sit down with them or ever accept something they gave to you.'

As to answering exactly why some strangers aren't to be trusted, it's not necessary to go into detail. 'You could simply say, "There are some adults that may be mean to you or don't like children, so you must always tell me if someone you don't know does talk to you",' suggests Hayes. Try not to be too negative or melodramatic and always balance your explanation with what we know to be true; that the vast majority of adults are friendly, kind and well meaning – there is no reason for them to assume otherwise. As Hayes says, 'Don't scare them – it's much better that they learn how to be confident and independent, not terrified to answer the door.'

'Mummy, why is that lady dressed like Darth Vader?' Caitlin, 5

Reassure yourself that at five years old your child isn't trying to be derogatory – even though it may feel that way if you're standing next to a lady wearing a burqa in the playground. She is genuinely introducing a comparison that she finds familiar. Once any acute social embarrassment has passed, you can combat her initial query with something neutral such as, 'We all wear different clothes for different reasons – that's what makes us so unique.'

'Try and stay as matter of fact and simple as you can,' advises educational psychologist Kairen Cullen. 'Keep it concrete and familiar – if you're a churchgoer you can talk about the robes that a priest or vicar wears and talk about their similarities. All the better if you can impart some knowledge, pitching it at the right angle so your child can learn and make sense of other cultures.' You could mention that when a bride walks down the aisle she wears a veil, and this relates to modesty as well as custom. In the same way, Caitlin wouldn't walk out of the house without her pants, socks, skirt or jeans on – it's no different for the lady dressed in black, you could tell her.

You can offer some simple, digestible facts about the burqa: that it's an outer garment worn by women in some Islamic traditions and that their equivalent of the Bible, the Qur'an, requires men and women to dress modestly in public life, a practice called 'hijab'.

Caitlin's question is a good opportunity to introduce the idea that people around the world dress differently for a variety of reasons, and that diversity is something to be enjoyed and celebrated. 'It's important for them to know early on that these cultural differences are unique but not odd. That positive distinction is key,' says Dr Susan Marchant-Haycox, a psychologist specialising in cross-cultural relations. You could explain that the colours we wear can symbolise different things in different countries. 'In China, for instance, wearing red, green and yellow is thought to bring you good luck,' she says. In Egypt black symbolises re-birth and, in many eastern cultures, white symbolises bad luck and death.

Beyond culture, you can bring it back to the more accessible realm of practicality. 'Depending on where you're from, black covering protects against the elements; the sun and the wind, as well as the cold,' says Marchant-Haycox. 'Even wearing black kohl around the eyes is thought to protect the skin it is covering.' At which point you can chat about what it would be like if we travelled to other parts of the world, and what people might think of *our* clothes – what do we wear, you could ask, that could seem unique and unusual to others? 'You can also explain that where we live – England – is very special because it is so richly diverse,' says Marchant-Haycox. 'You could say, "Wouldn't it be dull, Caitlin, if we all looked the same?"'

'Mummy, what is a Chav?'
Ryan, 11

How you answer Ryan's query will depend largely on how you feel about the term yourself. You may think, like many people, that it is snobby and insulting, and puts those that use such a term in a much worse light than the group it is aimed at; young white, working-classes with a supposed penchant for branded fashion, sportswear and gold jewellery.

Yet the term is now so well established – it first appeared in mainstream dictionaries in 1995 – you may as well accept that your child will come across it sooner or later. Rather than expressing immediate disapproval, which will only make the term more exciting to them, open up his question for general discussion.

You could offer Ryan a literal definition and tell him that the *Oxford English Dictionary* suggests 'chav' may come from the Romany term 'Chavo', for boy or 'Chatham girls' – referring to the town in Kent. Others think it's how Cheltenham College schoolgirls snobbishly referred to young men in the town: 'Cheltenham Average.'

You could then ask Ryan what *he* thinks it means and talk about various definitions. There are some people, like Lee Bok, author of *The Little Book of Chav Speak*, who feel that chav is simply a neutral description: 'It's just a word that quickly describes a social set, no different from mods, rockers or hippies,' he maintains. 'It's Britain's designer-hoody-wearing, unemployed elite who like wearing plenty of Burberry and Calvin Klein. It's not snobby; really it's an easy handle to describe a certain youth group, generally between ten to 30 years old.' You could ask Ryan if he agrees with this claim or whether he feels the term is rather more judgemental than this, and, if so, why?

You may be ignorant to actually use such a term but to fully understand it does require a relatively sophisticated level of knowledge about prejudice and the British class system. You could suggest that other people find it highly insulting – writer Julie Burchill, for example, describes the term as 'social racism' – and discuss why this may be. Suzie Hayman, agony aunt and trustee for Parentline Plus says, 'The first thing I'd say is, "Chav makes assumptions and gives a picture of what a person is like that isn't accurate. It's saying, they dress in a certain way so they must be a bit of a no-hoper and they don't work." I'd then ask, "Can what someone wears and where they live really say all that about them?"'

Try not to be too critical – let them work out its derogatory implications. You can also talk about the humorous potential of

172

comic characters like *Little Britain*'s Vicky Pollard and Catherine Tate's Lauren ('Am I bovvered?'). You could ask your child why they found, or still find, them amusing? Do they ever make them feel uneasy? Do they think they're accurate?

Asking questions, rather than simply defining the term, is the best way forward, agrees Dr Pat Spungin, founder of raisingkids.co.uk. 'I would also add that chav is *always* used in a derogatory sense, it can never be positive, and ask them, really, how that can be a good thing?'

Don't worry that Ryan has alighted on a negative term. Reassure yourself it is extremely positive that, at the age of 11, he's come to you for honest answers and not his friends – make the most of it because perhaps next time he won't.

'Mummy, why do some parents smack their children?' Eleanor, 9

If Eleanor is asking this question, it is fair to assume that her own parents don't advocate smacking themselves. In which case, you would want to reassure Eleanor that this is not about to change. 'If they see it, they may worry you might do the same thing,' says Eileen Hayes, parenting advisor to the NSPCC. 'It's important to point out that you wouldn't and that although you don't believe in it, some parents feel that if they smack their children, they'll behave better.' At which point, you could ask Eleanor what she feels about parents smacking their children – is it something she agrees with? If Eleanor were naughty, heaven forbid, what does she think Mum and

Dad should do to punish her?

You could also ask her, how would she do things differently? You may be surprised at her response. 'You quite often find that children would be far more punitive than you are,' says child development psychologist Elaine Douglas. 'They'll often come up with quite extreme punishments like, "I'd ground them for two years."' This is partly because of their stage of cognitive development. 'Until 11 years old and onwards, most children will still view smacking as very good or very bad because they're at that stage of development where everything is concrete, black or white.' It is good if you can discuss the concept of smacking in reasonable terms. Even if you are against it, it's important to introduce them to the idea of complexity and grey areas.

You could say, 'We may not agree with smacking but this is why it happens; sometimes parents get frustrated. They don't have the patience to sit down and go through issues with the child. Or they don't have the same attitudes as our family.' You can throw in that much American research confirms that children who haven't been smacked tend to behave better. 'We know that positive parenting produces good behaviour in children,' says Hayes. 'A good ratio is six positives to every negative; those negatives aren't just smacking but a whole range of behaviours including sarcasm and putting a child down verbally.'

You could discuss with Eleanor alternative punishments, such as going without pocket money or being sent to her bedroom – does she feel they are preferable? If so, why? It is an interesting way of encouraging Eleanor to think about the nature of authority and punishment, as well as other parenting styles. It will also invite her to look at the nature of right and wrong in society. 'They do have to learn that the world isn't always a fair place where people behave in a kind and equable way,' says Douglas. Much easier, though, to absorb this bitter but essential truth from the vantage point of not being smacked themselves.

'Why does Archie live in a bigger house than us – does that mean we're poorer?'
Daniel, 8

If this is a question you've secretly pondered yourself, along with coveting Archie's mothers' brand new Poggenpohl kitchen, then maybe you shouldn't be too surprised that Daniel has raised the question. Remember, how you react initially will speak volumes to him about your own material aspirations – to some extent he will be influenced. Thus, the more we compare ourselves in material terms, the more our children will too. Bob Reitemeier, chief executive of The Children's Society says, 'The real point about materialism is that we have to look in the mirror. There's no question about it. It's really a cop out to blame children for being materialist – they only learn from us.'

Of course, it's not all our fault. He also believes that with an estimated £30 billion market in which children make purchases or influence family spending, commercialisation encourages just these sorts of questions from our children. Even the mother of all recessions won't dent our relentlessly acquisitive society. So how to tackle it? Reitemeier recommends using such a question as a point for reflection about happiness in general. 'I would frame it along the lines of, "When did you feel most content?"' suggests Reitemeier. 'Help them reflect on what happiness means; how it's almost always more to do with people – being with family and friends – than material wealth,' he says. 'You could also say that, personally, you choose to purchase a house that helps to build and make the family happy, not necessarily just because it's big. And, frankly, a big house isn't the answer.' Which is quite possibly a lesson that's easier to learn as we see house prices falling.

Vocalising that fact may offer you some comfort too. Also, reassuringly, it's not just a materialistic society that shapes your child – or you for that matter. 'Around the age of eight years old, children will make comparisons because they always have done. It's important to realise this is when children are beginning to position themselves in the wider world outside the family; they're noticing differences,' says child development specialist Elizabeth Hartley-Brewer. Differences that have little bearing on their material desires. So it's not necessarily a sense of unfairness that would provoke this question, just a healthy, instinctive curiosity. In which case, says Hartley-Brewer, keep your answer factual and simple. 'I would say, a big bar of chocolate costs more than a small one and big cars cost more than small cars, so some possessions cost more than others and it really depends what you choose to spend your money on.'

Whatever you do, don't apologise for the fact that your house is smaller than Archie's, advises Hartley-Brewer. 'Otherwise they'll feel it's lacking too. It's important to suggest there are choices and it's not about being poor – you want to get across that you've got all the money you need to feel happy.' If you can convince yourself this is true, then Archie may just about believe it too.

'Mummy, what's the point of voting?'
Sasha, 14

You could say, 'Look no further than Barack Obama, the first American African president in power. It is the enthusiasm of first time voters, many of them black and female, that helped to get him there. For the first time ever, they used their vote and brought about incredible change.'

Even though it's difficult to imagine which candidate here could fire up first time voters to such a degree, the principle still remains. Young, female American voters wanted to change their country and the only way they could do that was with their vote. Another reason, you could tell Sasha, is 'civic duty' – a justification Professor Susan Banducci, head of politics at the University of Exeter, gave to her nine year old who asked a similar question during the last American election. 'I told her that civic duty was the most important reason; together you can make a decision about leadership. It's your duty to other citizens for the collective good. Every person has an equal opportunity to express their voice in an election – if they don't vote, they lose that voice.'

Or as MP Tony Benn puts it, 'I think the saying, "Take an interest in politics before politics takes an interest in you" is very true, ie. before politics sends your loved ones to war or takes their jobs away, decide who to vote for.'

Voting raises your profile – even if you don't feel you can make a significant change to government, you will register on their radar and you won't be so easily overlooked. In other words, through electoral research, politicians know who votes for them in terms of age, gender, profession etc – and their policies will be influenced accordingly. Banducci, who studies electoral behaviour, says, 'The reason I give my daughter is that if you're not a potential voter, politicians won't pay attention to you. Vote and your issues get onto the agenda.' Which is why politicians are keener to appeal to female voters these days because they're aware, says Banducci, that 'women tend to vote more than men do; they turn out in higher numbers'.

You could then tell Sasha how we shouldn't take the female vote for granted – that women have only been allowed to vote since 1918, thanks to the dogged activism and personal sacrifice of the suffragette movement. How would she feel, you could ask her, if all the boys she knew could vote but she wasn't allowed to? Would that make her more or less bothered about using her vote?

You could also talk to Sasha about why you vote, who you've voted for and why you felt it was worth the effort. Politics can seem quite abstract to a young person so try and introduce issues that feel closer to home; how would she feel if her school closed down, for instance, or if her local MP planned to build a sewer in the local park.

MP Tony Benn adds, 'I would always encourage your children to become interested in issues and the idea of campaigning. Progress is made by people who campaign; so start getting involved in whatever you feel strongly about; then you'll get drawn in and realise that there has to be a political system to get those issues implemented.' Even if they're too young to get involved, at least they can work out the connection between issues that are personal to them and the more distant world of Westminster. If that doesn't convince Sasha, you could always quote Benn: 'You could say voting is important because it's the one way you can get rid of governments without having to kill anyone.' A civilised system indeed.

'Mummy, why do women show their bosoms in magazines?'
Lewis, 8

Let's hope Lewis is referring to mainstream magazines rather than any other sort of publication. As adults we're pretty much inured to the sexualised images of women, particularly in advertising. It is only when you see a child flicking through the pages of a fashion magazine that you begin to realise what a stark contrast the pictures present to them, how different and artificial the images must seem. Lewis may question them now but within four years he'll begin to view it as entirely normal, and desirable. This is a good opportunity to discuss the influence of advertising. 'You could talk about the way that advertising appeals to women, who buy more products than men, making us believe that if we buy whatever they're selling, we'll look more like the person in the picture,' suggests Dr Helen

Haste, professor of psychology at University of Bath. 'You can go on to point out that what is on offer in these pictures is a world of excitement, attractiveness, glamour which becomes associated with that product.'

Although this doesn't quite address exactly why some of these women are semi-clad. 'And that is where it gets more complicated,' admits Haste. It may be difficult to explain to an eight year old the relationship between sex, aspiration and consumption. 'You could say that advertisers think it's more attractive to look at people who show their bodies – and people like beautiful-looking bodies.'

By eight years old, Lewis will be highly aware of advertising aimed at children, from computer games to films, soft drinks and toys. The world of adult commercialisation will still be something of a mystery – but not for long. 'They need to be aware of how important gender is here,' says Dr Ruth Cherrington, a lecturer in cultural and media studies at University of Warwick. 'That women's bodies do still sell more than men's, that they are sexualised as a commodity. The media reinforces fairly traditional stereotypes and it starts at a young age.'

You could talk to Lewis about the difference in marketing; what sort of toys are sold to girls and boys and why he thinks this may be. Is it advertising that dictates their tastes – princesses and prams for girls, super heroes and weapons for boys – or the other way round? 'I think it's so important to make them aware of what's going on,' says Cherrington. 'Ideally media literacy should be part of the school curriculum so we can increase their awareness and give them a better understanding.' You could easily begin at home by looking through some of the pictures that Lewis has seen and talking about them in depth. 'It would be an interesting way way of asking him what he thinks we mean by beauty, how this relates to what real people look like,' says Haste. 'You could take them from adverts to looking at pictures of women in art, how beauty is important in all cultures and the way it changes through the ages.'

As Cherrington says, 'Children can be media savvy with encouragement.' A recent copy of *Vogue* is as good a place to start as any.

In case of difficulty in purchasing any Short Books
title through normal channels, please contact
BOOKPOST Tel: 01624 836000
Fax: 01624 837033
email: bookshop@enterprise.net
www.bookpost.co.uk
Please quote ref. 'Short Books